DRESSINGS
AND MARINADES

Classic and novel ways to
enliven every dish

HILAIRE WALDEN

CHARTWELL
BOOKS, INC.

A QUINTET BOOK

Published by Chartwell Books
A Division of Book Sales, Inc.
114 Northfield Avenue
Edison, New Jersey 08837

This edition produced for sale in the U.S.A., its
territories and dependencies only.

ISBN 0-7858-0555-9

This book was designed and produced by
Quintet Publishing Limited
6 Blundell Street
London N7 9BH

Creative Director: Richard Dewing
Designer: Ian Hunt
Senior Editor: Laura Sandelson
Editor: Gail Dixon Smith
Photographer: David Armstrong

Typeset in Great Britain by
Central Southern Typesetters, Eastbourne
Manufactured in Singapore by
Eray Scan (Pte) Ltd
Printed in Singapore by
Star Standard Industries (Pte) Lte

CONTENTS

INTRODUCTION

Salad dressings and marinades are both easy ways of making food more exciting and interesting, highlighting its intrinsic flavor, complementing it or giving it new flavor. They can both be flavored in an almost infinite number of ways using ingredients from around the world.

Salad Dressings

Salad dressings are vital to the success of a salad; they can make it by adding a touch of originality, freshness, or distinction, or spoil it by being insipid, inappropriate, or overdone. A salad dressing can transform simple ingredients into a special treat, vegetables into an exotic dish.

Try to match the ingredients of a dressing to the salad ingredients. For example, Walnut Dressing (see page 61) blends excellently with a pear and blue cheese salad and adds an extra, complementary flavor and texture; Basil Dressing (see page 43) has a natural affinity to a simple summery salad of sliced, well-flavored sun-ripened tomatoes.

However good a dressing, do not add so much that the salad ingredients are drowned.

The two most widely used salad dressings are the simple French Dressing (see page 18) and mayonnaise (see page 19). Historically this has been a troublesome sauce to make because unless care is taken when making it, it will curdle or fail to thicken. But now, thanks to blenders and food processors, homemade mayonnaise can be made with greater assurance, and more quickly (see page 19). It is still necessary though, to make sure all the ingredients are at room temperature and not to add the oil too quickly. Unless you have a small blender or food processor bowl, a two egg yolk/1¼ cup oil quantity is the minimum that can be made because the blender or processor blades must be covered by the egg yolks

when starting to make the sauce. Should mayonnaise curdle while you are making it, put another egg yolk, at room temperature, in a clean bowl then very gradually add the curdled mixture, whisking constantly.

Many different dressings can be made using a basic French dressing-type mixture or mayonnaise. For example, the character can easily be varied enormously by using different types of oil and vinegars or fruit juices such as lemon, lime, and orange, the type of mustard as well, and of course, by adding flavoring ingredients such as herbs, spices, garlic, and shallots, producing a vast repertoire of recipes with flavors as diverse as Chinese, Indian, Thai, East meets West, Mexican, Middle Eastern, Italian, and Greek.

Try to make a salad dressing about 30 minutes before it is to be used to allow the flavors to develop, although herbs are best not added until the last moment as they can discolor. Whisk French dressing-type dressings again before using. Thin dressings are usually used for leaf salads while thicker dressings are more suitable for mixing with firmer textured ingredients such as potatoes and chicken.

A dressing is usually added to leaf salads, except cabbage, immediately before being served, otherwise the leaves wilt. Cooked vegetables such as potatoes, pasta, beans, and broiled eggplants are usually mixed with the dressing while they are warmed then left to cool, so they absorb the flavors of the dressing. Raw ingredients such as sliced mushrooms are also sometimes left to marinate for a while in the dressing.

Salads are not the only foods that salad dressings can be used with. They can also be served over or with plain broiled, baked and roasted meat, poultry, game, fish, and vegetables.

Marinades

Marinades are used on food before cooking to give it flavor, prevent it from drying, and to tenderize meat, game, poultry and, to a lesser degree, fish.

Marinades can be divided into three groups – wet marinades, pastes and dry or spice rubs.

A wet marinade is a well-flavored liquid in which food is steeped. It will contain an acid such as wine, vinegar, plain yogurt or fruit juice, a little oil; and flavoring such as herbs or spices. The amount of oil will depend on how the food is to subsequently be cooked; marinades for broiling usually contain at least 25 per cent oil whereas there will be much less in marinades for casseroles.

There are two main types of wet marinade: uncooked and cooked. Uncooked marinades are used for tender or relatively tender foods such as chicken, pork, fish, and vegetables, and cuts of lamb and beef for broiling, frying, or roasting. Most marinades made nowadays are uncooked.

Cooked marinades are usually wine-based and are used for red meats and game. Before cooking the marinated food, drain the food and dry it thoroughly otherwise it will not brown. An exception to this rule is food marinated in yogurt. The remaining marinade is often used in the cooking of the dish.

A paste is a thick mixture that is spread in an even layer over food that is to be broiled, roasted, or baked. Not only will a paste provide a protective coating during cooking, but when left to marinate, it will penetrate food, giving it additional flavor and tenderizing foods such as meats and fish. During cooking, pastes often develop a crisp crust with a delicious slightly caramelized or smoky-taste.

Dry marinades, or spice rubs, are blends of herbs, usually dried, and spices that are rubbed into meat, poultry, game, and fish. The herbs and spices are lightly crushed together in a mortar and pestle (or with the end of a rolling-pin in a bowl). The food should be dried thoroughly first then rubbed with oil before the spice rub is applied. It is then left to marinate before cooking.

Salt is not added to marinades for meats, game, poultry, and fish because it draws out their juices.

The container used for marinating should be made from a non-reactive material such as glass and it should not be too large. The longer a food is left in a marinade, the more flavor it will absorb and the greater the tenderizing effect; and the flavor of foods at room temperature will develop twice as fast as those in the refrigerator. Slashing the food will hasten penetration of the marinade so reducing the marinating time. The smaller the piece of food and the more delicate its texture, generally the shorter the marinating time. The food should be completely covered by the marinade and stirred or turned during the marinating time.

Foods that are left in the refrigerator to marinate should be returned to room temperature about 30 minutes before cooking, depending on the size of the food and the length of time refrigerated.

Ingredients for Salad Dressings

EGGS – some eggs have been shown to contain salmonella so the elderly, young, babies, pregnant women, and people with poor immune defence systems are advised not to eat raw or lightly cooked eggs.

GARLIC – garlic is nearly always used raw in dressings and marinades, so it really is important that firm cloves that are as fresh as possible are used. Ideally, the cloves should not have green sprouts growing out of their tops, but if they do, be sure to remove all of the sprout as it tastes bitter.

Buy garlic that feels firm, is shiny with the paper skin still attached, not peeling off in flakes. Store garlic in a cool, dark, airy place.

The intensity of the garlic flavor varies according to how the cloves are prepared. For salad dressings, it is best to mince the cloves with a small dash of salt because, not only does chopping give a harsher flavor than crushing them, but many people do not like to bite on small pieces of raw garlic.

Another way to add a mild garlic flavor to a salad dressing is to roast the cloves (see page 70).

To give a mild garlic flavour to a salad, the salad bowl can be rubbed with a cut clove of garlic.

HERBS – all the recipes in this book have been made using fresh herbs, except where dried ones are mentioned as in the spice rubs. With the exception of the rubs, I never use dried herbs. If I do not have the fresh herb I want growing in my garden, either in the ground or in a pot, in a window box or in a pot on the windowsill (a surprising number of herbs can be grown successfully in tubs, window boxes and pots on windowsills) and I am unable to buy fresh herbs, I buy frozen or freeze-dried herbs, which most supermarkets now stock. Many supermarkets and greengrocers also sell herbs growing in pots.

Store fresh herbs in "stay-fresh" bags in the refrigerator.

Fresh herbs can vary quite considerably in flavor, so it is important to taste each batch you are using and adjust the amount you use as necessary.

OILS – oils are the foundation of most salad dressings and are an important addition to marinades because they add flavor to the food being marinated, lubricate it and keep it moist during cooking (see pages 10–12).

PEPPER – along with salt, pepper, usually black, is the common seasoning for salad dressings. White pepper may be used where dark specks of black pepper would spoil the appearance of a recipe.

To give your salad dressings the best flavor use freshly ground peppercorns rather than ground pepper as this is too fine and powdery and lacks the fresh piquancy of freshly ground corns.

SALT – many experienced cooks prefer to use sea salt or other coarse salts, believing their flavor to be superior to ordinary table salt, but at a recent tasting of a wide selection of different salts, involving food writers and chefs, the salt that came out on top was regular salt!

SOY SAUCE – now used not only in Chinese and Japanese cooking, but also in other recipes to add depth to the flavor, as well as a characteristic taste.

Light Soy Sauce – this is light in color but it has a full flavor and is more salty than dark soy sauce. In Chinese food stores light soy sauce is known as Superior Soy. It is the sauce that is generally used for cooking; the word "light" may not always be included.

Dark Soy Sauce – this is matured for longer than light soy sauce so has a darker color. Its flavor is slightly stronger than light soy sauce and it is slightly thicker. It is known as Soy Superior Sauce in Chinese food stores, and is the one most often sold there. Its most common use is in dipping sauces.

SPICES – for the best flavor, use freshly ground spices rather than ready ground ones. To get the maximum flavor from the whole spices, before grinding them, heat them gently in a heated heavy skillet until they smell fragrant.

Because the flavor of spices deteriorates with age, buy spices in small amounts that you will use quickly; if you have any for more than 6 months, throw them away. Keep the spices in a cool, dark, dry place.

SZECHUAN PEPPERCORNS – reddish brown color and a sharp, mildly spicy flavor that has a hint of lavender. Szechuan peppercorns do not come from the same family as white, black, and green peppercorns and do not have the same "hotness". Szechuan peppercorns are usually dry roasted and ground before using to bring out their full flavor.

VINEGAR – vinegar is the second most important ingredient in salad dressings and marinades, after oil. Vinegar is important in both dressings and marinades for adding flavor and piquancy, and in dressings it is important for forming an emulsion with the oil, so thickening the sauce, while in marinades it tenderizes meat, poultry, game, and fish (see pages 13–15).

Oils

Oils flavored with aromatics such as herbs and spices are useful for instantly adding flavor to a dressing. All oils should be kept in a cool, dark place. Mild oils should then keep fresh for 6–9 months; olive oils, nut oils, and sesame oil should be used within 4–6 months, the better the quality of an olive oil, the more quickly it should be used.

Olive Oil – there is now a burgeoning range of olive oils of different styles and qualities. The descending order of quality, purity, intensity of flavor, and price of the grades is:

EXTRA VIRGIN OLIVE OIL – from the first pressing of the olives. This has the lowest acidity and the most rounded flavor. Commercially produced extra virgin oils are blended from oils of differing character and quality and will always taste the same. Extra virgin oils from estates, farms, and village co-operatives have their own individual characters and, as they are unblended, will vary from year to year in the same way as wine. These oils are used in salads and marinades where a rich olive taste is wanted, or when only small quantitites of oil are required.

VIRGIN OLIVE OIL – the result of the second pressing of the olives. Virgin olive oils are used for salad dressings where a less pronounced but still discernible olive flavor is required, and more widely in cooking.

SIMPLE OLIVE OIL – or pure olive oil – a blend of virgin olive oil and refined olive oils obtained by chemical extraction. It is used for salad dressings and marinades where the taste of the oil should be barely noticeable.

Within each category, there is a range of flavors. Oils from different countries, areas and producers can range from delicate and grassy to full, heavy, and fruity. Spanish oils tend to be lighter than Italian ones, whereas Greek oils are even heavier because the olives are allowed to become very ripe before they are picked.

Color is not an indication of quality, but a rich dark green oil does indicate a strength of flavor.

CORN OIL – also goes under the name of maize oil. It is quite bland but has a slight smell and taste (which some people find unpleasant) so is more suitable for cooking than making salad dressings.

GRAPESEED OIL – a pale oil with a mild nutty taste. It makes good salad dressings.

PEANUT OIL – also known as ground nut or arachide oil, has a light texture and a pleasant, mild, unobtrusive taste which makes it a good all-purpose oil. In salad dressings and marinades it is useful when the flavor of choice ingredients needs to show through. Peanut oil found in Asian food stores has a stronger taste of peanuts and is more expensive.

SAFFLOWER OIL – a pale, bland oil that is very high in polyunsaturates, which are believed to break down cholesterol. Safflower oil is good for cooking and mild salad dressings.

SESAME OIL – is a thick, rich, golden brown oil made from sesame seeds, which give it a distinctive nutty flavor and aroma. Sesame oil made from toasted seeds is darker and has a richer, toasted flavor so is used in small quantities mixed with milder oils.

SUNFLOWER OIL – lighter than corn oil but slightly more cloying and robustly flavored than peanut oil, it makes a good, all-purpose oil.

VEGETABLE OIL – is a blend of oils from various vegetable products, such as soya, rapeseed or canola, palm, and coconut. (Check individual labels for precise details.) Vegetable oils are usually cooking oils.

WALNUT AND HAZELNUT OILS – have full, rich tastes and aromas so are best used in combination with olive oil or a mild oil. Nut oils are particularly good with bitter salad greens and mushrooms. Nut oils become rancid more quickly than other oils so it is adviseable to buy them in small quantities and it is even more essential to keep them in a cool, dark place.

Flavored Oils

These are oils that have herbs steeped or soaked in them. They have long been used in Mediterranean, Indian, Chinese, and other Asian cooking. It is best to buy infused oils that have been commercially prepared because preparing infused oils at home, especially those oils containing garlic and onion, can promote the growth of botulism. Commercially prepared and with the proper preservatives, however, these oils can be considered perfectly safe – and delicious. They should be refrigerated after opening:

A store-bought infused oil can liven up a vinaigrette. Or you can dip dense bread into flavored oil for an imaginative alternative to butter. Flavored oil can also provide the perfect complement to pasta, pizza, or bruschetta. Infused oil can top a baked potato or substitute for butter and milk to make garlicky mashed potatoes. You could also try sautéeing fresh artichoke hearts in an infused oil, or drizzling a little over poached salmon, broiled eggplant, roasted peppers, or other vegetables. A low-fat or non-fat prepared mayonnaise can also be jazzed up with a little infused oil.

Types of Vinegars

Balsamic vinegar – is a special Italian red wine vinegar that has been aged in barrels for a number of years; the longer the maturing the darker the color, the more intense the sweet-sharp flavor, and the higher the price. Only a few drops of this vinegar are needed when using in dressings, but of the cheaper, though not cheap, commercial balsamic vinegars you will need to use a little more.

Cider vinegar – mild, slightly sweet, apple flavor.

Distilled white vinegar – too strong and dominantly flavored to use for dressings and marinades.

Flavored vinegars – such as tarragon, raspberry, garlic or chile instantly add flavor to a dressing. Flavored vinegars are very easy to make at home (see pages 14 and 15).

Malt vinegar – this brown vinegar, like distilled vinegar, is unsuitable for salad dressings and marinades.

Rice vinegar – this is made from rice. There are two main types of rice vinegar.

WHITE RICE VINEGAR – is clear with a delicate flavor that has a slight nuance of glutinous rice. It has a low acid content, so is mild, therefore, to give piquancy to a recipe, you will need to add more white rice vinegar than you would white wine vinegar.

BLACK RICE VINEGAR – an inky black Chinese rice vinegar that has a rich, spicy fragrance.

Japanese rice vinegar has a smoother, more mellow, almost sweet taste compared to Chinese rice vinegar, which is sharper.

Sherry vinegar – is made from the grape most used in sherry making and is aged in old sherry casks which give it a unique, rich, sweetish, sherry-like flavor. Like balsamic vinegar, sherry vinegar should be used more like a seasoning than an acidifier.

Wine vinegars – the quality of wine vinegars varies considerably but price is usually a good guide; Orleans wine vinegars are the best but only one company, Martin Pouret, still makes them. Red wine vinegar has a stronger flavor than a white wine vinegar of the same brand.

Flavored Vinegars

Herb Vinegars

Most culinary herbs can be used to make flavored vinegars – tarragon, rosemary, thyme, marjoram, parsley, basil, bay, fennel, dill, and sage. They can be used either individually or as a mixture.
Use fresh, preferably freshly picked, herbs. Pick herbs in the morning of a dry day, after the dew has disappeared but before the sun is too hot, and select sprigs on which flowers have not formed.

METHOD

Bruise the herbs lightly to release their flavor and pack into a jar or bottle so that it is half-filled. Pour in white or red wine vinegar to fill the jar or bottle and seal tightly with non-reactive tops.

Shake the bottle or jar and leave in a cool dark place for 2–3 weeks, shaking every day.

Strain the vinegar, pressing down well on the herbs. Taste the vinegar to see if the herb flavor is strong enough. If it is not, repeat the process. A fresh herb sprig can be added to the prepared vinegar, if liked.

Garlic Vinegar

MAKES ABOUT 3 CUPS

INGREDIENTS	
12 plump garlic cloves	garlic cloves for garnish (optional)
3 cups white wine vinegar	

METHOD

Lightly crush the garlic cloves and put them into a jar or bottle. Pour in the vinegar, cover and shake the jar or bottle. Leave in a cool, dark place for 2–3 weeks.

If the flavor of the vinegar is strong enough, strain it and re-bottle. If liked, thread 2–3 garlic cloves per bottle onto a wooden toothpick and add to each bottle.

Herbes de Provence Vinegar

MAKES ABOUT 3 CUPS

INGREDIENTS	
3 large sprigs of tarragon	4 bay leaves
3 large sprigs of thyme	dash of fennel seeds
3 sprigs of rosemary	3 cups white wine vinegar

METHOD

Lightly bruise the herbs then pack into a jar or bottle. Pour in the vinegar and close tightly. Shake the jar or bottle and leave in a cool dark place for 2–3 weeks, shaking the jar or bottle daily.

Strain the vinegar, pressing down well on the herbs. Taste the vinegar to see if the herb flavor is strong enough. If it is not, repeat the process. A fresh herb sprig can be added to the prepared vinegar, if liked.

Fruit Vinegars

MAKES ABOUT 2 CUPS

For a few years fruit vinegars seemed to appear in all manner of recipes, irrespective of whether they really contributed anything beneficial to the dish. Now, thank goodness, moderation and sense have prevailed. Use this vinegar, which has quite a concentrated flavor, to add an interesting fruity flavor to dressings for rich meats such as duck or game and salads containing fruit.

INGREDIENTS	
1 lb fruit such as raspberries, strawberries, or black currants	2 cups white wine vinegar ¼ cup sugar

METHOD

Put the fruit into a non-metallic bowl or jar, add a little of the vinegar and crush the fruit with the back of a wooden spoon to release the juice. Add the remaining vinegar, cover and leave in a cool place for 1 week, stirring occasionally.

Strain the vinegar into a saucepan, add the sugar and heat gently, stirring until the sugar has dissolved. Bring to a boil. Cool.

Pour the vinegar into a clean bottle, cover and store in a cool, dark place.

Orange Vinegar

MAKES ABOUT 4¼ CUPS

INGREDIENTS	
3 large oranges	1 small orange
4¼ cups white wine vinegar	

METHOD

Thinly pare the rind from the 3 large oranges, taking care not to include any white pith. Put the rind into a clean large jar. Cut the 3 oranges in half and squeeze out the juice. Pour into the jar, seal and shake. Leave in a cool, dark place for 3 weeks, shaking the jar occasionally.

Strain the vinegar and re-bottle. Thinly pare some of the rind from the small orange so no pith is included. Cut the rind into thin strips and add 3 strips to each bottle.

1

CLASSIC
SALAD DRESSINGS

Some salad dressings such as French Dressing and Mayonnaise are classics in their own right and can be used with a number of different type of salads whereas others, such as Caesar Salad Dressing and Tuna Mayonnaise are most often associated with particular salads; this does not mean that they cannot be combined with other salad ingredients. Tuna Mayonnaise, which partners *Vitello Tonnato* (cold poached veal) also marries well with boiled eggs, chicken, and crisp green salad leaves.

French Dressing

MAKES 5 TBSP.

French dressing (or vinaigrette to use the French name) is a simple combination of oil, vinegar, and seasoning, whisked together until the oil and vinegar have emulsified and the dressing has thickened. The usual proportions of oil to vinegar are about 3–4:1 but this can be varied according to the acidity of the vinegar, how sharp you want the dressing to be and the composition of the salad. Mustard, usually Dijon, is an optional flavoring, usually in the proportion of ½ tsp. to 3–4 parts oil and 1 part vinegar, but it will also help an emulsion to form. Use whatever type of oil you prefer. The basic dressing, without the optional garlic, will keep for as long as 1 month in a screw-top jar in the refrigerator.

French dressing can be used over a limitless number of salad ingredients.

INGREDIENTS

3–4 Tbsp. oil	½ tsp. *Dijon* mustard (optional)
1 Tbsp. white wine vinegar	salt and freshly ground black pepper

METHOD

Put all the ingredients into a bowl and whisk together until emulsified and thickened.

Mayonnaise

MAKES 1½ CUPS

INGREDIENTS

2 egg yolks
(see page 8)

about 1 tsp. *Dijon*
mustard

2 Tbsp. white wine
vinegar or lemon juice

1¼ cups oil

salt and freshly ground
white or black pepper

The keys to success when making mayonnaise are having all the ingredients at room temperature and adding the oil very slowly, especially at first, and whisking all the time.

Whether you use all olive oil, half olive oil and half a bland oil such as sunflower oil, or all of a bland oil is a matter of personal taste. For extra character, use a proportion of a nut oil. The choice of wine vinegar or lemon juice is also a question of individual taste and the use to which the sauce is to be put.

Homemade mayonnaise can be kept in a covered container in the refrigerator for up to 3 days. If the mayonnaise becomes too thick during this time, stir in a little water to thin it.

METHOD

Put the egg yolks into a bowl and stir in half of the vinegar or lemon juice, and the mustard.

Add the oil, drop by drop, whisking constantly. After about half of the oil has been incorporated the rest can be added slightly more quickly but continue to whisk, until all the oil has been emulsified and the sauce is thick and shiny.

Beat in the remaining vinegar or lemon juice and season to taste; add more mustard, if liked.

Blender Mayonnaise

Put the egg yolks, mustard, seasoning, and half of the vinegar or lemon juice into a blender or food processor and mix together briefly at low speed until blended. With the motor running, slowly pour in the oil in a thin, steady stream to make a thick, emulsified sauce. Add the remaining vinegar or lemon juice.
NOTE: when making mayonnaise in a blender or food processor 1 whole egg rather than 2 egg yolks can be used, which will make a lighter sauce.

Caesar Salad Dressing

MAKES ABOUT 1 CUP

Caesar salad was invented in Tijuana, Mexico by Caesar Cardini. During the Prohibition era Americans flooded over the border to his restaurant in search of hard liquor which they were unable to get at home. The salad was later popularized in the New York restaurant Chasens, and is now available across the nation. Needless to say, there are quite a number of versions of the dressing.

INGREDIENTS

3 garlic cloves	about 6 Tbsp. virgin olive oil
2 egg yolks (see page 8)	½ cup freshly grated Parmesan cheese
1 tsp Worcestershire sauce	salt and freshly ground black pepper
1 Tbsp. lemon juice	

METHOD

Mash the garlic with a dash of salt in a bowl using the end of a rolling pin. Whisk in the egg yolks, Worcestershire sauce, and lemon juice.

Slowly pour in the oil, whisking constantly until well emulsified. Stir in the cheese then season to taste.

Boiled Salad Dressing

MAKES ABOUT 1½ CUPS

This old-fashioned dressing is useful for those who do not like oil. It goes well with shredded celeriac and cabbage, green and vegetable salads, and eggs.

INGREDIENTS

3 Tbsp. all-purpose flour	¾ cup milk
1 tsp. dry mustard powder	2 Tbsp. melted butter
1 Tbsp. sugar	4 Tbsp. white wine vinegar
dash of cayenne pepper	salt and freshly ground black pepper
2 egg yolks	

METHOD

Mix the flour, mustard powder, sugar, and cayenne pepper together in a saucepan. Stir in the milk, egg yolks, butter, and vinegar until evenly mixed then heat very gently, whisking constantly, until thickened and smooth.

Season to taste and let cool, stirring occasionally to prevent a skin forming.

ABOVE *Caesar Salad Dressing*

Remoulade Sauce

MAKES ABOUT 2 CUPS

This robustly-flavored recipe is for the classic remoulade sauce, which really adds life to cold meats, eggs, fish, and boiled vegetables, turning them into appetizing salads. As an alternative you could mix in celeriac, mustard, and lemon juice to make celeriac remoulade.

INGREDIENTS

1½ cups mayonnaise, bottled or homemade (see page 19)

2 tsp. *Dijon* mustard

3 Tbsp. pickles, chopped

3 Tbsp. capers, chopped

3 Tbsp. chopped fresh parsley

1 Tbsp. chopped fresh tarragon

4 anchovy fillets, chopped

METHOD

Put the mayonnaise into a bowl. Stir in the remaining ingredients.

Blue Cheese Dressing

MAKES ABOUT 1½ CUPS

Some people include a proportion of mayonnaise in this favorite salad dressing, but this is the version I prefer because it is lighter, yet has a creamy taste and texture. The better the blue cheese the better the dressing; Roquefort is a traditional cheese to use and I also find Stilton and Gorgonzola make a good dressing, but Danish Blue is too harsh. Blue cheese dressing is used on and with many foods, from salad leaves to jacket potatoes.

INGREDIENTS

3 oz. blue cheese, crumbled

1 garlic clove, finely crushed (optional)

1 cup sour cream or rich yogurt

about 1 Tbsp. white wine vinegar

about 2 Tbsp. chopped fresh parsley, or 1 Tbsp. chopped chives (optional)

freshly ground black pepper

METHOD

Mash the cheese and garlic, if used, with a fork. Mix in the sour cream or yogurt, the vinegar, and parsley or chives, if using. Season with black pepper; because of the saltiness of the cheese, extra salt should not be necessary.

Cover and set aside in a cool place, but not the refrigerator if possible, for several hours. Stir before serving.

Green Goddess Dressing

MAKES ABOUT 2 CUPS

A play starring the English actor George Arliss provided the name for this dressing, which was invented at the Palace Hotel in San Francisco (the hotel was destroyed in the earthquake and fire of 1906). Although it is now usual to include sour cream in the dressing, it did not feature in the original recipe. Use the dressing for fish, shellfish, or vegetable salads.

INGREDIENTS

1 cup mayonnaise, bottled or homemade (see page 19)

½ cup sour cream

1 garlic clove, finely chopped

3 anchovy fillets, finely chopped

4 Tbsp. finely chopped fresh parsley

4 Tbsp. finely chopped chives

1 Tbsp. lemon juice

1 Tbsp. tarragon vinegar

salt and freshly ground black pepper

METHOD

Put all the ingredients into a bowl and stir together.

Thousand Island Dressing

MAKES ABOUT 1½ CUPS

The islands to which the title refers are in the St. Lawrence Seaway on the Canadian border. The original 19th-century dressing did not contain mayonnaise but was simply a vinaigrette dressing flavored and colored pink by paprika pepper or tomato paste, Serve with crisp green salads, egg, potato, or shrimp salads.

INGREDIENTS

1 cup mayonnaise, bottled or homemade (see page 19)

2 Tbsp. stuffed olives, finely chopped

1 Tbsp. finely chopped green pepper

1 Tbsp. finely chopped onion or chives

1 Tbsp. chopped fresh parsley

1 hard-cooked egg, finely chopped

few drops of Tabasco sauce

salt and freshly ground black pepper

METHOD

Put the mayonnaise into a bowl. Stir in the remaining ingredients.

Sauce Vierge
(Tomato and Olive Oil Dressing)

MAKES ABOUT 1½ CUPS

For this dressing you really should have well-flavored, sun-ripened tomatoes and good quality olive oil. When the sauce is left to infuse for 30 minutes there is no need for the saucepan to be over heat. The dressing goes well with all types of salads and can also be served with broiled fish or cold chicken, turkey, and fish.

RIGHT *Thousand Island Dressing*

INGREDIENTS

4 well-flavored tomatoes, peeled and seeded

2 small garlic cloves, unpeeled

scant 1 cup virgin olive oil

2 Tbsp. chopped fresh basil or chervil

2 Tbsp. chopped parsley

1 Tbsp. chopped tarragon or thyme

8 coriander seeds, roasted and crushed (see page 12)

salt and freshly ground black pepper

METHOD

Cut the tomatoes into ¼ inch dice and put into a bowl. Stir in the remaining ingredients.

Put the bowl over a saucepan of hot water, cover and leave for 30 minutes. Remove from the pan and leave until cold.

Coleslaw Dressing

MAKES ABOUT 1⅓ CUPS

Caraway seeds, a classic complement to cabbage, give this creamy dressing for the ever-popular raw cabbage salad, an extra touch of distinction.

INGREDIENTS

½ cup sour cream

½ cup mayonnaise, bottled or homemade (see page 19)

5 Tbsp. cider vinegar

1 tsp. mustard powder

2 tsp. caraway seeds

dash of fine granulated sugar

salt and freshly ground black pepper

METHOD

Put the sour cream, mayonnaise, vinegar, mustard powder, and caraway seeds in a bowl. Whisk together until evenly combined. Add sugar and seasoning to taste.

Salad Cream

MAKES ABOUT 1 CUP

This is a traditional English creamy, cooked salad dressing. It is served with potato or any other vegetable salads, egg salads, or with fish or cold chicken. Only the yolks are used, after hard-cooking the whole eggs; the whites can be chopped and used in salads or sandwiches.

The dressing should be made about 2–2½ hours in advance as it needs time in the refrigerator to thicken to the consistency of thickish cream.

INGREDIENTS

3 eggs	4 tsp. white wine vinegar
1 Tbsp. water	cayenne pepper
⅔ cup heavy cream	salt

METHOD

Put the eggs into a saucepan and cover with cold water. Bring to a boil then boil for 9 minutes. Drain the eggs and rinse under cold running water.

Peel the eggs and remove the whites. Put the egg yolks and water into a bowl and pound together with a wooden spoon to make a smooth paste. Slowly add the cream, stirring well after each addition. Stir in the vinegar and add cayenne pepper and salt to taste. Cover and refrigerate for 2–2½ hours, after which time it will have thickened.

Sauce Louise

MAKES ABOUT 1¾ CUPS

This zesty sauce is particularly associated with stuffed artichokes, shrimp, and crab.

INGREDIENTS

1 cup mayonnaise, bottled or homemade (see page 19)	4 tbsp. chopped green onions
¼ cup heavy cream	4 Tbsp. chopped green pepper
2 Tbsp. lemon juice	few drops of Tabasco sauce
1 tsp Worcestershire sauce	

METHOD

Put the mayonnaise into a bowl. Stir in the cream and lemon juice, then the remaining ingredients.

ABOVE *Russian Dressing*

Russian Dressing

MAKES ABOUT 2 CUPS

The original Russian dressing recipe contained caviar, hence the name. Serve it with green salads, vegetables, eggs, shellfish, or cold meats.

INGREDIENTS

1½ cups mayonnaise, bottled or homemade (see page 19)

4 Tbsp. tomato catsup

4 Tbsp. pickles, chopped

1 shallot, finely chopped

1 tsp. grated fresh horseradish

few drops of Tabasco sauce

METHOD

Put the mayonnaise into a bowl. Stir in the remaining ingredients.

Sauce Gribiche

MAKES ABOUT 1½ CUPS

This sauce is made like mayonnaise and although it is now often made using raw egg yolks, originally, as in this recipe, cooked ones were used. Stir into boiled vegetables to turn them into delicious salads, spoon over halved hard-cooked eggs or serve with cold meats, poultry, or fish that are served with a simple green salad.

INGREDIENTS

2 hard-cooked eggs

2–3 tsp. *Dijon* mustard

1¼ cups sunflower or mild olive oil

2 Tbsp. white wine vinegar

1 Tbsp. capers, chopped if large

1 Tbsp. chopped fresh tarragon

1 Tbsp. chopped fresh parsley

1 Tbsp. chopped chives

1 Tbsp. chopped gherkins (optional)

finely grated rind of ½ lemon

salt and freshly ground black pepper

METHOD

Separate the egg whites from the yolks; reserve the whites for garnishing. Sieve the yolks and stir in the mustard.

Add the oil to the egg yolks, drop by drop, beating constantly as when making mayonnaise. After half of the oil has been incorporated, the rest can be added slightly more quickly. Stir in the remaining ingredients.

Aioli

MAKES ABOUT 1½ CUPS

Aioli is a type of mayonnaise which has puréed garlic cloves as a base. It comes from Provence, where it is also sometimes known as "beurre de Provence". An imitation Aioli can be made using bottled or homemade mayonnaise (see page 19) by crushing the garlic and salt then gradually stirring in the prepared mayonnaise.

INGREDIENTS

6–12 garlic cloves

salt and freshly ground
black pepper

2 egg yolks (see page 8)

½–1 tsp. *Dijon* mustard
(optional)

about 1¼ cups olive oil

1½ Tbsp. lemon juice or
white wine vinegar, or a
combination of the two

METHOD

Put the garlic and a dash of salt into a mortar or bowl and crush them together until reduced to a paste. Work in the egg yolks, and mustard if using.

Add the oil, a few drops at a time, while stirring slowly, evenly and constantly. After half of the oil has been incorporated, add half of the lemon juice or vinegar. The rest of the oil can now be added a little more quickly but the sauce must be stirred in the same way.

Add the remaining lemon juice or vinegar and season.

Tuna Mayonnaise

MAKES ABOUT 1½ CUPS

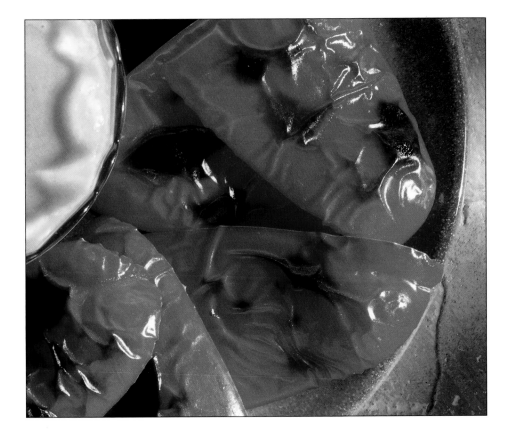

Tuna mayonnaise is the classic sauce to spoon over the Italian dish of poached veal, Vitello Tonnato, but it is so delicious that it has many other uses. For example, it perks up potato, tomato, red pepper, zucchini, plain, crisp green, fish and shellfish salads, and goes a treat with hard-cooked eggs and avocados. For extra zest and depth of flavor, add some chopped capers and anchovy fillets; tarragon vinegar can be used instead of lemon juice.

INGREDIENTS

1 small garlic clove	1 egg or 2 egg yolks
½ cup canned tuna, drained	1½ tsp. *Dijon* mustard
about 2 Tbsp. lemon juice	1 cup olive oil
leaves from a sprig of parsley	½ cup sunflower oil
	salt and freshly ground black pepper

METHOD

Put the garlic, tuna, lemon juice, parsley, egg, and mustard into a blender. Mix together briefly to make a smooth paste. With the motor running, slowly pour in the olive oil then the sunflower oil until well emulsified and thick.

Season to taste and add more lemon juice if liked.

2

SALAD DRESSINGS WITH HERBS

A couple of tablespoons or so of fragrant fresh herbs are all that is needed to add vibrancy to simple salad dressings, giving them new life so that they immediately add an extra air of quality to a salad.

The type of herb you use can change the character of a salad; oregano, for example, can impart a sunny southern Italian flavor, whereas if you use mint a salad will have a clean, clear taste.

Herbs tend to darken after a little while in a salad dressing, so it is best not to add them until shortly before you are going to use the dressing.

Mint and Tomato Vinaigrette

MAKES ABOUT 1 CUP

Quickly make a warm pasta salad with this chunky dressing, or use it to make an interesting salad out of cooked chicken or turkey. It is also good over salad leaves, with avocado or zucchini salads, or served with warm fish such as tuna, salmon, red mullet or, more humbly, fresh mackerel.

INGREDIENTS

scant ½ cup olive oil	1 shallot, finely chopped
1 tsp. white wine vinegar	3 well-flavored tomatoes
1½ tsp. lime juice	1 Tbsp. chopped fresh mint
1 garlic clove, finely chopped	salt and freshly ground black pepper

METHOD

Put all the ingredients except the tomatoes and mint, into a bowl and whisk together until well emulsified.

Peel, seed and chop the tomatoes. Stir the tomatoes and mint into the dressing and season to taste.

Herb Vinaigrette

MAKES ABOUT ½ CUP

Either a single herb or a combination of herbs can be used, but try to choose ones that are complementary to the salad ingredients. If you are making the dressing in advance, do not include the herbs until shortly before it is to be served otherwise they may darken. A well-flavored herb vinaigrette can happily be included as part of any salad.

INGREDIENTS

2 Tbsp. white wine vinegar or lemon juice	1 tsp. *Dijon* mustard (optional)
salt and freshly ground black pepper	6 Tbsp. olive oil
	2 Tbsp. chopped fresh herbs

METHOD

Put the vinegar or lemon juice, seasoning, and mustard, if used, into a bowl. Slowly pour in the oil in a thin steady stream, whisking until the vinaigrette has emulsified and thickened. Taste for seasoning and the level of herbs and adjust if necessary.

Special Parsley and Lemon Dressing

MAKES ABOUT ¾ CUP

If possible, make the dressing a few hours or even a day ahead and leave it in a cool place, preferably not the refrigerator. Mix again before using in salads with crisp lettuce leaves, such as Romaine, and croutons.

INGREDIENTS

⅔ cup virgin olive oil

2 Tbsp. lemon juice

1 tsp. grated lemon zest

2 garlic cloves, finely chopped

2 tsp. chopped parsley

1 tsp. sherry vinegar

1½ Tbsp. freshly grated Parmesan cheese

salt and freshly ground black pepper

METHOD

Mix all the ingredients together until well emulsified.

Oregano and Anchovy Dressing

MAKES SCANT 1 CUP

I suggest using this dressing for broiled eggplants, peppers, zucchini, and onions, with tomato or green salads, or with broiled fish. A small blender can also be used to make the dressing: put the soaked anchovy fillets, garlic, herbs, and half the lemon juice into the blender or food processor and mix briefly. With the motor running, very slowly trickle in the oil until the dressing is well emulsified. Switch off the machine and add the sun-dried tomatoes and black pepper.

INGREDIENTS

3 oz. canned anchovy fillets	juice of 1 lemon
little milk	5 Tbsp. virgin olive oil
1 small garlic clove, minced	1 tsp. sun-dried tomatoes in oil, finely chopped
1½ Tbsp. finely chopped fresh oregano	freshly ground black pepper

METHOD

Soak the anchovy fillets in milk for 5 minutes, then drain.

Put the anchovy fillets into a mortar with the garlic and herbs and crush together with a pestle to make a smooth paste, slowly working in half of the lemon juice.

Beat in the oil a drop at a time until half has been added. Stir in the remaining lemon juice then slowly trickle in the remaining oil, beating constantly. Lightly stir in the chopped sun-dried tomatoes and season with black pepper.

Pesto Vinaigrette

MAKES GENEROUS 1 CUP

The addition of pesto sauce quickly makes an interestingly-flavored dressing that is also versatile; it goes with green, pasta and nearly all vegetable salads (beet is one exception I've found), and with egg, shellfish, chicken, turkey, and beef salads.

INGREDIENTS

5–6 Tbsp. white wine vinegar	⅔ cup olive oil
4 tsp. pesto sauce	salt and freshly ground black pepper

METHOD

Put 5 Tbsp. of the vinegar and the pesto sauce into a bowl. Slowly pour in the oil, whisking until emulsified.

Season to taste and add more vinegar if liked.

RIGHT *Oregano and Anchovy Dressing*

Tarragon and Sesame Dressing

MAKES SCANT ½ CUP

With its nutty taste, this dressing complements sliced, well-flavored ripe tomatoes. In place of the sesame oil you could use walnut oil.

INGREDIENTS

4 tsp. chopped fresh tarragon

1 Tbsp. *Dijon* mustard

2 Tbsp. lemon juice

2 Tbsp. sesame oil

dash of sugar (optional)

salt and freshly ground black pepper

METHOD

Put all the ingredients into a bowl and whisk together.

Parsley Dressing

MAKES ABOUT 1 CUP

The flavor of parsley does not vary much from season to season, so this is a useful, and welcome, herb dressing for the winter, especially as it happily combines with winter vegetable salads. To make the dressing in a small blender or food processor, put the garlic, fennel seeds, and a dash of salt into the machine, mix briefly then, with the motor running, slowly pour in the oil, adding 2 Tbsp. of the parsley towards the end. Pour into a bowl and stir in the remaining parsley, the green onions, tarragon, and black pepper.

INGREDIENTS

2 garlic cloves

¼ tsp. fennel seeds

salt and freshly ground black pepper

leaves from a large bunch of parsley

about 2 Tbsp. white or red wine vinegar

rind of 1 lime, finely grated

¾ cup olive oil

3 green onions, finely chopped

1 tsp chopped fresh tarragon (optional)

METHOD

Put the garlic, fennel seeds, and a dash of salt into a mortar or bowl. Crush together with a pestle or the end of a rolling-pin until reduced to a paste, adding 2 Tbsp. of the parsley towards the end.

Stir in the vinegar and lime rind. Slowly trickle in the oil, whisking until well emulsified.

Stir in the remaining parsley, the green onions and tarragon, and season with black pepper.

Tomato and Basil Dressing

MAKES ABOUT 1¼ CUPS

A light, clean-tasting dressing for fish and shellfish, pasta, egg, chicken, or avocado salads. The walnut oil enhances the flavor of the tomatoes and if you are able to use well-flavored, sun-ripened tomatoes they should be sweet enough for the dressing. If not, add a little sugar.

INGREDIENTS

1 Tbsp. olive oil

2 Tbsp. walnut oil

2 Tbsp. white wine vinegar

1 Tbsp. sherry vinegar

3 well-flavored tomatoes

18–20 basil leaves, chopped

dash of fine granulated sugar (optional)

salt and freshly ground black pepper

METHOD

Pour the oils and vinegars into a bowl. Whisk together.

Peel, seed and finely chop the tomatoes then stir into the dressing with the basil. Add a little sugar if necessary, then season to taste.

ABOVE *Chive and Lemon Vinaigrette*

Chive and Lemon Vinaigrette

MAKES ABOUT ¾ CUP

Use this dressing to make a delicious, light potato salad by tossing it with warm potatoes, particularly new ones, and finely chopped green onions, then leaving until cold.

INGREDIENTS

1 garlic clove

salt and freshly ground black pepper

4 Tbsp. lemon juice

rind of 1 lemon, finely grated

1½ tsp wholegrain mustard

4 Tbsp. virgin olive oil

2 Tbsp. chopped chives

METHOD

Put the garlic and a dash of salt into a bowl. Crush together, then stir in the lemon rind and juice, and the mustard until smooth.

Slowly pour in the oil, whisking constantly, until well emulsified.

Add the chives and season with black pepper.

Herb, Lemon, and Caper Dressing

MAKES ABOUT 1¼ CUPS

This dressing goes well with shellfish, green, cucumber, zucchini, or egg salads, or with broiled fish, especially salmon or firm fish such as monkfish or fresh cod, and fish cakes.

INGREDIENTS

½ garlic clove

salt and freshly ground black pepper

4 Tbsp. lemon juice

4 Tbsp. capers

2 Tbsp. chopped chives

2 Tbsp. chopped dill

⅔ cup olive oil

METHOD

Put the garlic and a dash of salt into a mortar. Crush together with a pestle until reduced to a paste.

Stir in the lemon juice, capers, and herbs. Slowly trickle in the oil, whisking until well emulsified. Season with black pepper.

Herb, Garlic, and Mustard Dressing

MAKES ABOUT 1 CUP

This is a quite strongly flavored dressing so is best used for more robust salads such as salade Nicoise.

INGREDIENTS

1–2 garlic cloves	leaves and fine stems from a small bunch of chervil
salt and freshly ground black pepper	1 tsp. *Dijon* mustard
leaves from 4–5 sprigs of thyme	¼ cup red wine vinegar
	¾ cup olive oil

METHOD

Put the garlic, a dash of salt, and herbs into a bowl. Crush together then stir in the mustard and the vinegar until smooth.

Slowly pour in the oil, whisking constantly, until well emulsified. Season with black pepper.

Basil Dressing

MAKES ABOUT ¾ CUP

I love basil but as it is always at its best when it has basked in glorious sunshine, I reserve making this dressing until the summer. Then I use it for many salads, such as warm pasta, shellfish, green, potato, zucchini, egg, cheese, and broiled vegetables.

INGREDIENTS

2 garlic cloves	1 Tbsp. white wine vinegar
leaves from 1 large bunch of basil	6 Tbsp. virgin olive oil
salt and freshly ground black pepper	2 Tbsp. freshly grated Parmesan cheese

METHOD

Put the garlic, basil leaves, dash of salt, and vinegar into a small blender. Mix briefly then, with the motor running, slowly pour in the oil until well emulsified.

Transfer to a bowl. Stir in the cheese and season with black pepper.

Cilantro, Caper, and Lime Dressing

MAKES ABOUT 1 CUP

Try tossing this piquant dressing with warm potatoes or celeriac then letting cool, or use for seafood salads, or spoon over fried foods such as fish or sliced cheeses such as feta.

INGREDIENTS

1 garlic clove, finely chopped	4 Tbsp. virgin olive oil
1½ tsp wholegrain mustard	3–4 Tbsp. capers
finely grated rind and juice of 2 limes	3 Tbsp. chopped fresh cilantro
1 Tbsp. white wine vinegar	freshly ground black pepper

METHOD

Put the garlic, mustard, lime rind, juice, and vinegar into a bowl and mix together. Slowly pour in the oil, whisking constantly, until well emulsified. Stir in the capers and cilantro. Season with black pepper.

3

SALAD DRESSINGS
WITH SPICES

Aromatic spices from around the world add their magical touch to salad dressings. These then quickly turn simple salad ingredients into exotic treats. The salads do not have to be authentically ethnic but can be made of any ingredients you like.

Black Bean, Ginger, and Watercress Dressing

MAKES ABOUT ⅔ CUP

If you do not have any rice wine, you can use 1 Tbsp. rice vinegar and 1 Tbsp. water instead. Serve with fish salads made of salmon or firm white fish such as monkfish, chicken, young spinach leaves, warm Chinese egg thread, or cellophane noodles.

INGREDIENTS

1 Tbsp. salted black beans, coarsely chopped	2 tsp. grated fresh ginger
1 Tbsp. groundnut or grapeseed oil	2 Tbsp. rice wine
2 tsp. sesame oil	1½ oz. fine stems and leaves of watercress
	freshly ground black pepper

METHOD

Steep the black beans in 1–2 Tbsp. hot water for 15 minutes. Drain and dry on paper towels.

Put the black beans, oils, ginger, and rice wine into a bowl and whisk together until emulsified. Stir in the watercress and season with black pepper.

Chile and Ginger Dressing

MAKES SCANT ½ CUP

Use this zesty dressing to dress pork, beef, chicken, duck, or fish salads.

INGREDIENTS

¾ cup grapeseed or groundnut oil	1 inch piece fresh ginger, grated
2 Tbsp. white wine vinegar	2 green onions, finely chopped
1–2 fresh green chiles, seeded and finely chopped	salt and freshly ground black pepper

METHOD

Whisk together the oil and vinegar until emulsified.

Add the chiles, ginger, and green onion. Mix together then season to taste.

Nutty Cilantro Dressing

MAKES ABOUT 1¾ CUPS

As this is a dark sauce it is appropriate for serving over dark leaves such as radicchio and oak leaves. It also marries well with warm Asian noodle salads or stir-fried vegetable salads.

INGREDIENTS

5 Tbsp. peanut oil

2 Tbsp. sesame oil

5 Tbsp. chopped cilantro

4 Tbsp. light soy sauce

4 Tbsp. red wine vinegar

3 Tbsp. crunchy peanut butter

3 Tbsp. black bean sauce

2 oz. fresh ginger, grated

2 tsp. chili sauce

1 Tbsp. fine granulated sugar

METHOD

Put all the ingredients into a food processor and mix until smooth. Alternatively, beat together in a bowl.

Chile and Cilantro Vinaigrette

MAKES ABOUT 1 CUP

Containing chiles, ground cumin and fresh cilantro this dressing is an obvious candidate for using over Mexican-style bean and corn salads.

INGREDIENTS

3 fresh green chiles, seeded and finely chopped

½ tsp. ground cumin

2 Tbsp. cider vinegar

salt

½ cup peanut oil

leaves from a small bunch of cilantro, chopped

METHOD

Put the chiles, cumin, vinegar, and salt into a bowl. Whisk together. Slowly pour in the oil, whisking constantly, until the dressing is well emulsified. Stir in the cilantro just before serving.

Coconut and Peanut Dressing

MAKES ABOUT ¾ CUP

To roast the Szechuan peppercorns, see page 51, then grind them in a spice grinder or crush them very finely in a mortar and pestle. Serve over Chinese noodle salads or raw vegetable salads.

INGREDIENTS

1½ Tbsp. groundnut oil

2 garlic cloves, minced

2 oz thick coconut milk

4 tsp. soy sauce

2 Tbsp. rice vinegar

3 Tbsp. peanut butter

good dash of soft dark brown sugar

large dash of ground roasted Szechuan peppercorns

freshly ground black pepper

METHOD

Heat the oil in a small heavy skillet, add the garlic and fry gently for 1–2 minutes. Add the coconut and stir gently. Stir in the remaining ingredients until well mixed.

Ginger and Cilantro Vinaigrette

MAKES ABOUT 1 CUP

The cilantro is added at the last minute otherwise it will darken. A garnish of toasted sesame seeds complements the dressing. Toss with salad leaves such as curly endive, Romaine, watercress or young spinach, use for cheese salads, or to dress fish such as sea bass, tuna or salmon, or for chicken or pork.

INGREDIENTS

½ inch piece of ginger, grated

1 shallot, finely chopped

juice of 1 lime

1 Tbsp. soy sauce

2 Tbsp. rice wine vinegar

½ cup olive oil

1 Tbsp. dark sesame oil

salt and freshly ground black pepper

½ bunch of cilantro, coarsely chopped

METHOD

Put the ginger, shallot, lime juice, soy sauce, and vinegar into a bowl and whisk together.

Trickle in the olive oil, whisking vigorously, then whisk in the sesame oil. Season to taste. Add the cilantro just before serving.

Indonesian Peanut Dressing

MAKES ABOUT 2 CUPS

This dressing is an essential part of the Indonesian mixed vegetable, tofu, and flat omelet salad, gado gado, although it is served separately rather than over the salad ingredients. It can also be served as a dressing for warm potato, green bean, cauliflower, zucchini, or celery salads. If the dressing is prepared in advance, it may separate: this can be rectified by heating gently and stirring in about 1 Tbsp. of water.

INGREDIENTS

2 Tbsp. groundnut oil	¾ cup coconut milk
1 onion, finely chopped	1½ tsp. soy sauce
1 garlic clove, finely minced	juice of ½ lime
dash of crushed red chiles	1 tsp. brown sugar
1 cup unsalted roasted peanuts	salt and freshly ground black pepper

METHOD

Heat the oil in a skillet, and fry the onion until lightly browned. Add the garlic and chiles and fry until the onion is golden.

Meanwhile, put the peanuts into a food processor and grind to a coarse paste. Stir in the coconut milk, soy sauce, lime juice, sugar, and nut paste, mixing well until smooth and creamy. Season.

Szechuan Peppercorn Dressing

MAKES ABOUT 1¾ CUPS

This dressing, which has quite a pronounced flavor, will lose its color, though not its flavor, if kept for more than a few hours. Serve it over duck, chicken, and cold pasta salads.

INGREDIENTS

1 Tbsp. Szechuan peppercorns	1 Tbsp. fresh parsley
3 garlic cloves	1 Tbsp. fresh dill
juice of 6 limes	1 Tbsp. sugar
1 Tbsp. fresh cilantro	salt and freshly ground black pepper

RIGHT *Indonesian Peanut Dressing*

METHOD

Put the peppercorns into a dry small, heavy skillet and heat until fragrant. Tip into a blender and add the remaining ingredients. Mix until smooth.

Curry Dressing

MAKES ABOUT ⅔ CUP

I use a medium curry paste; if you use a hot or mild one do not forget to adjust the amount to add to the dressing accordingly. The dressing gives character to salads containing fruit, or salads with watercress or spinach, or served over shrimp.

INGREDIENTS

1 tsp. curry paste	6 Tbsp. grapeseed or groundnut oil
1 garlic clove	about ½ tsp. grated fresh ginger (optional)
salt and freshly ground black pepper	
1½ Tbsp. white vinegar or lemon juice	

METHOD

Put the curry paste, garlic, and a dash of salt into a mortar or small bowl and crush together to a paste using a pestle or the end of a rolling pin.

Whisk in the vinegar, then slowly pour in the oil, whisking constantly until well emulsified.

Add the ginger, if liked, and season to taste with black pepper.

Sesame Dressing

MAKES 1 CUP

I use this dressing over Asian noodle salads that are served hot. Chinese egg noodles can be cooked in advance, cooled then kept covered in the refrigerator. Just before serving, reheat the noodles in a covered colander over a saucepan of boiling water for 5–7 minutes.

INGREDIENTS

3 Tbsp. peanut oil	½–1 fresh red chile, seeded and finely chopped
2 Tbsp. sesame oil	4 Tbsp. chopped fresh cilantro
4 Tbsp. soy sauce	
1 garlic clove, minced	
3 Tbsp. toasted sesame seeds	

METHOD

Mix together all the ingredients except the cilantro. Immediately before serving, add the cilantro leaves.

Satay Dressing

MAKES ABOUT 2¼ CUPS

If you cannot buy roasted unsalted peanuts, toast unsalted peanuts under the broiler until browned, stirring frequently so they brown evenly.

Serve the dressing over pork, beef, chicken or shellfish satays, or kebabs and garnish with lime wedges.

INGREDIENTS

¾ cup roasted unsalted peanuts	2 Tbsp. soft dark brown sugar
1 garlic clove	squeeze of lime juice
2 Tbsp. red curry paste	dash of hot chile powder
1¾ cups coconut milk	

METHOD

Put the peanuts, garlic, curry paste, and a little of the coconut milk into a blender and mix to a paste. Add the remaining coconut milk and sugar. Mix until smooth.

Pour the ingredients into a saucepan and add the lemon juice. Boil for 2 minutes then simmer gently for 10 minutes, stirring occasionally to prevent sticking. Add a little water if the sauce becomes too thick. Add chile powder to taste. Serve warm.

4

SALAD DRESSINGS
WITH FRUITS AND NUTS

———————

Fruits can be used in salad dressings in place of all or part of the vinegar and have the additional bonus of giving the dressing more flavor and character. Each fruit has its own special taste so if you make basically the same dressing with different fruits you will get quite different results.

Nuts contribute both flavor and texture to salad dressings. To maximize the flavor of nuts, spread them on a baking sheet and toast in a preheated oven at 350°F for 15–20 minutes, stirring the nuts occasionally, until they are brown and crisp. Buy nuts in small quantities and store them in a cool, dark place. Before using any nuts, make sure that they are absolutely fresh without any hint of rancidity.

Mango Vinaigrette

MAKES ABOUT 1¼ CUPS

Use this dressing to accompany smoked chicken, turkey, or pork.

INGREDIENTS

1 ripe mango, peeled and sliced	1 Tbsp. white wine vinegar
1 small to medium fresh red chile, seeded and chopped	½ cup olive oil
	salt and freshly ground black pepper

METHOD

Put all the ingredients into a blender and mix until smooth.

Orange Vinaigrette

MAKES ABOUT 1 CUP

Use this dressing to finish a refreshing salad of thinly sliced fennel and oranges, or a grated carrot salad. With a dash of caraway seeds added it can be used for beet salads.

INGREDIENTS

4 Tbsp. orange juice	1 tsp. balsamic vinegar
1 tsp. finely grated orange rind	1 shallot, finely chopped
1 Tbsp. white wine vinegar	6 Tbsp. virgin olive oil
	salt and freshly ground black pepper

METHOD

Put all the orange juice and rind, the vinegars, and shallot into a bowl. Slowly pour in the oil, whisking until well emulsified. Season to taste.

Lemon Vinaigrette

MAKES ABOUT ¾ CUP

Lemon rind and juice give this dressing a good lemony flavor. It is especially good for fennel or endive salads.

INGREDIENTS

1 garlic clove	juice of 1 large lemon
salt and freshly ground black pepper	¼ tsp. paprika pepper
finely grated rind of ⅓ large lemon	dash of cayenne pepper
	6 Tbsp. virgin olive oil

METHOD

Put the garlic and a dash of salt into a mortar or bowl and crush together with a pestle or the end of a rolling pin until reduced to a paste.

Stir in the lemon rind and juice, the paprika, and cayenne pepper. Slowly pour in the oil, whisking until well emulsified.

Roast Tomato and Garlic Vinaigrette

MAKES ABOUT ¾ CUP

Pour the dressing over broiled red peppers, zucchini, eggplant, and onions, or toss with pasta.

INGREDIENTS

1 large ridged tomato	4 Tbsp. virgin olive oil
3 plump garlic cloves, unpeeled	salt and freshly ground black pepper
1 tsp. sherry vinegar	

METHOD

Preheat the broiler. Broil the tomato and garlic until softened, charred and blistered. Let cool then peel them. Seed and chop the tomato.

Put the garlic and tomato into a blender and mix until smooth. Add the vinegar then, with the motor running, slowly pour in the oil until well emulsified. Season.

Poppy Seed Vinaigrette

MAKES ABOUT 1 CUP

The light nutty crunch of the poppy seeds adds a fillip to avocado salads, green salads of leaves such as chicory, and savory fruit salads.

INGREDIENTS

½ tsp. English mustard powder	1 Tbsp. clear honey
¼ tsp. ground ginger	1 Tbsp. poppy seeds
½ red onion, grated	⅔ cup peanut oil
3 Tbsp. red wine vinegar	salt and freshly ground black pepper

METHOD

Put the mustard powder, ground ginger, onion, vinegar, honey, and poppy seeds into a bowl. Whisk together.

Slowly pour in the oil, whisking constantly, until the dressing is well emulsified. Season to taste.

RIGHT *Roast Tomato and Garlic Vinaigrette*

Orange and Lemon Dressing

MAKES ABOUT 1 CUP

Carrot and beet salads marry well with this quite complex flavored dressing, as do salads that contain fruit.

INGREDIENTS

finely grated rind and juice of 1 orange

4 tsp. lemon juice

¼ tsp. fennel seeds, crushed

1 tsp. balsamic vinegar

3 green onions, white parts only, finely chopped

salt and freshly ground black pepper

5 Tbsp. olive oil

1 Tbsp. hazelnut oil

3 Tbsp. mixed chopped herbs such as chervil, parsley, and chives

METHOD

Put the orange rind and juice, the lemon juice, fennel seeds, vinegar, green onions, and salt into a bowl and mix together. Slowly pour in the oils, whisking until well emulsified. Add the herbs and season with black pepper.

Creamy Orange and Hazelnut Dressing

MAKES ABOUT ¾ CUP

This dressing works a treat over a salad of broiled salmon with lamb's lettuce, spinach, watercress, or it can just be served over the salad leaves without the salmon. It also complements beet, carrot, fennel, and endive salads.

INGREDIENTS

3 Tbsp. orange juice

2 Tbsp. sherry vinegar

2 Tbsp. heavy cream

1 Tbsp. orange liqueur (optional)

scant ½ cup hazelnut oil

½ cup hazelnuts or filberts, toasted and chopped

salt and freshly ground pepper

METHOD

Put the orange juice, vinegar, heavy cream, and liqueur into a bowl. Mix together. Slowly pour in the oil, whisking, until the dressing emulsifies.

Add the hazelnuts and season to taste.

Walnut Dressing

MAKES ABOUT ½ CUP

Balsamic vinegar adds richness to the dressing; the amount you will need to add will depend on the richness of the vinegar and how richly flavored you want the dressing to be. For a lighter taste use some white wine vinegar in conjunction with the balsamic vinegar. Walnut dressing has a particular affinity with cheese, watercress, and spinach salads, and also harmonizes with cabbage and firm salad leaves.

INGREDIENTS

¼ cup walnut halves

3 Tbsp. olive oil

3 Tbsp. walnut oil

2 Tbsp. balsamic vinegar

salt and freshly ground black pepper

METHOD

Preheat an oven to 350°F. Spread the nuts on a baking sheet and put in the oven for about 15 minutes until crisp and browned. Chop the nuts. Put the oils and vinegar into a bowl. Whisk until well blended.

Add the nuts and season to taste.

Mediterranean Dressing

MAKES ABOUT 1 CUP

Bursting with the heat-soaked flavors that result from basking in the Mediterranean sunshine, this dressing is ideal for a salad made of cubed firm white bread (flavored with herbs or garlic if liked) and crisp salad leaves. It is also good spooned over broiled cheese, or tossed with pasta.

INGREDIENTS

2 oil-soaked sun-dried tomatoes	1½ Tbsp. red or white wine vinegar
1 small garlic clove	7 Tbsp. virgin olive oil
1 Tbsp. capers	dash of sugar (optional)
about 8 pitted black olives	freshly ground black pepper

METHOD

Finely chop the tomatoes, garlic, capers, and olives.

Put into a bowl and add the vinegar. Slowly pour in the oil, whisking constantly, until well emulsified. Season with sugar, if using, and black pepper.

Rich Sun-dried Tomato Dressing

MAKES ABOUT 1 CUP

Warm pasta salads benefit from tossing in this richly flavored dressing. It also adds life to potato salads and barbecued corn.

INGREDIENTS

4 oil-soaked sun-dried tomatoes	4 Tbsp. oil from the jar of sun-dried tomatoes
1 plump garlic clove	5 Tbsp. extra virgin olive oil
about 2 tsp. wholegrain mustard	salt and freshly ground black pepper
4 Tbsp. red wine vinegar	
2 Tbsp. sun-dried tomato paste	

METHOD

Put the sun-dried tomatoes, garlic, mustard, vinegar, and paste into a blender. With the motor running, slowly pour in the sun-dried tomato oil and the olive oil and mix briefly. Season to taste and add more mustard, if liked.

ABOVE *Mediterranean Dressing*

Lemon and Lime Cream Dressing

MAKES ABOUT 1½ CUPS

Lighter than mayonnaise (and without egg yolks) this clean-tasting dressing can be used as an alternative to mayonnaise to dress shrimp, scallop, and lobster salads, or chicken or turkey salads.

INGREDIENTS

finely grated rind and juice of 1 large lime

finely grated rind and juice of ½ lemon

4 plump green onions, finely chopped

salt and freshly ground black pepper

2 tsp. fine granulated sugar

5 Tbsp. olive oil

⅔ cup heavy cream

few drops of Tabasco sauce

METHOD

Put the lime and lemon rinds and juices, the green onions, salt, and sugar into a bowl. Slowly trickle in the oil, whisking until well emulsified.

Gradually whisk in the cream. Add Tabasco sauce and black pepper to taste.

Sweet and Savory Dressing

MAKES ABOUT 1 CUP

Use this dressing for fruit salads served as a first course, such as mixed melons. Chopped mint, grated fresh ginger, or a sprinkling of ground cinnamon are good finishing touches.

INGREDIENTS

2 Tbsp. clear honey

5 Tbsp. port

juice of 3 lemons

salt and freshly ground black pepper

METHOD

Put the honey, port, and lemon juice into a bowl. Stir together then season to taste.

Coconut and Lemon Dressing

MAKES ABOUT 1 CUP

Serve with fish or shellfish or Chinese noodle salads. Garnish the salad with basil leaves.

INGREDIENTS

1 Tbsp. groundnut or grapeseed oil

6 oz of creamed coconut, chopped

2 Tbsp. rice wine

3 inch piece of lemon grass, crushed and thinly sliced

large dash of five spice powder

salt and freshly ground black pepper

METHOD

Heat the oil in a small heavy skillet. Add the coconut cream and heat gently, stirring, until it has melted. Stir in the remaining ingredients until evenly blended.

5

MAYONNAISE-BASED
DRESSINGS

Mayonnaise is the second universally most well-
known salad dressing after French dressing.
Mayonnaise is most often served plain but there are so
many ways in which it can easily be flavored to make
excitingly different sauces to enliven salads – I have
not yet found a herb or spice that cannot be blended
with mayonnaise to good effect. Even vegetables such
as watercress (see page 68) can be added, or you can
add flavor and color by blending mayonnaise with
puréed cooked spinach or puréed broiled red peppers.

Homemade mayonnaise is very easy to make (see
page 19) but you may prefer to use bottled mayonnaise.
The somewhat lifeless flavor of bottled mayonnaise
can be improved by beating in a couple of tablespoons
of virgin olive oil, as well as other flavorings.

Simple Flavored Mayonnaises

ABOVE *Watercress Mayonnaise*

Watercress Mayonnaise

Remove the tough stems from a bunch of watercress. Chop the leaves and fine stems and add to 1½ cups homemade mayonnaise (see page 19), or bottled mayonnaise.

Chantilly Mayonnaise

Whip 5 Tbsp. whipping or heavy cream until it stands in soft peaks then gently fold into 1½ cups homemade mayonnaise (see page 19), or bottled mayonnaise.

Horseradish Mayonnaise

Add 1–2 Tbsp. lemon juice and 2 Tbsp. freshly grated horseradish to 1½ cups homemade mayonnaise (see page 19), or bottled mayonnaise.

Herb Mayonnaise

Add about 6 Tbsp. chopped fresh herbs to 1½ cups homemade mayonnaise (see page 19), or bottled mayonnaise.

Caper Mayonnaise

Add 4 tsp. chopped capers and 1 tsp. tarragon vinegar to 1½ cups homemade mayonnaise (see page 19), or bottled mayonnaise.

Extra Light Mayonnaise

Whisk 1–2 egg whites until they form stiff peaks then fold into 1½ cups homemade mayonnaise (see page 19), or bottled mayonnaise.

Light Mayonnaise

Stir together yogurt and homemade mayonnaise (see page 19) or bottled mayonnaise in the proportions you want. I particularly like to use a rich yogurt for this.

Lemon Mayonnaise

If making homemade mayonnaise (see page 19), use lemon juice rather than vinegar, and add 2 Tbsp. finely grated lemon rind to the egg yolks. If using bottled mayonnaise, add the grated lemon rind to the mayonnaise.

Sauce Verte

MAKES 1½ CUPS

A favorite dressing for cold summer platters of fish, especially salmon, or poultry. The dressing also complements hard-cooked eggs and many cold, boiled vegetables. I use it in egg and chicken sandwiches.

INGREDIENTS

4 oz. mixed herbs and leaves, such as sorrel, watercress, and spinach	1½ cups bottled or homemade mayonnaise (see page 19)

METHOD

Add the herbs and leaves to a saucepan of boiling water and boil for 30 seconds. Drain and rinse under cold running water. Drain well and squeeze dry.

Chop finely or purée in a blender. Add the herbs and leaves to the mayonnaise. Cover and chill.

Roast Chile and Szechuan Peppercorn Mayonnaise

MAKES SCANT 1½ CUPS

This dressing is not as thick as regular mayonnaise. It can be used to lend an Asian flavor to all manner of salads.

INGREDIENTS

4 oz. fresh red chiles	1 cup mild olive oil (or ½ cup olive oil and ½ cup groundnut oil)
2 egg yolks (see page 8)	
1 plump garlic clove	dash of roasted Szechuan peppercorns (see page 51)
salt	
2 Tbsp. orange juice	

METHOD

Preheat the broiler. Broil the chiles until the skins are charred and blistered. Let cool then peel off the skins, slice in half and discard the seeds.

Put the chiles, egg yolks, garlic, salt, and orange juice into a blender. Mix together briefly. With the motor running, slowly trickle in the oil. Add Szechuan pepper to taste.

Roast Garlic Mayonnaise

MAKES ABOUT 1½ CUPS

Roasting garlic softens its flavor and gives it a delicious smoky taste, which, in turn, adds an enticing flavor to the mayonnaise. If liked, 2 mashed anchovy fillets can be added with the egg yolks.

INGREDIENTS

2 garlic bulbs, unpeeled

2 sprigs of thyme or rosemary

2 Tbsp. olive oil

2 egg yolks
(see page 8)

2–3 tsp lemon juice

1¼ cups virgin olive oil

salt and freshly ground black pepper

METHOD

Preheat the oven to 350°F. Put each garlic bulb on a piece of wax paper. Add a thyme or rosemary sprig and trickle over 1 Tbsp. of olive oil. Fold up the wax paper to enclose the garlic and seal the edges together firmly to seal well. Put on a baking sheet and bake for 35–40 minutes until the garlic is soft.

Allow the garlic to cool slightly then squeeze the garlic cloves from their skins, into a bowl. Add the egg yolks and 1 tsp. of the lemon juice. Beat hard.

Beat in a drop of virgin olive oil at a time until half of the oil has been added. Add another 1 tsp. of lemon juice then slowly trickle in the remaining oil, beating hard, constantly.

Season and add more lemon juice, if necessary.

Saffron Mayonnaise

MAKES ABOUT 1½ CUPS

Saffron is expensive but only a few strands are needed to make this luxurious-tasting mayonnaise. It adds a real sense of occasion whenever· it is used with shellfish salads, for example. To make saffron mayonnaise from bottled mayonnaise, use 1 Tbsp. lemon juice and prepare the saffron in the same way. Add to bottled garlic mayonnaise.

INGREDIENTS

2 Tbsp. white wine vinegar	1 garlic clove
dash of saffron strands	salt and freshly ground black pepper
2 egg yolks (see page 8)	1¼ cups olive oil

METHOD

Pour the vinegar into a small saucepan. Boil for 2 minutes. Add the saffron, remove from the heat and let infuse for 5 minutes.

Put the egg yolks, saffron liquid, garlic and a dash of salt into a blender. Mix together. With the motor running, slowly trickle in the oil until well emulsified. Season with black pepper.

Piquant Cilantro Mayonnaise

MAKES ABOUT 1¼ CUPS

I like to serve this delightful dressing with jumbo shrimp, crab, lobster, chicken, potato, egg, or avocado salads or with broiled or fried lamb or fish and fish cakes.

INGREDIENTS

1 egg (see page 8)	4 small cornichons (continental dill pickles), finely chopped
1 small garlic clove	
½ tsp. English mustard powder	1½ Tbsp. small capers
salt and freshly ground black pepper	1 Tbsp. chopped fresh cilantro
¾ cup mild olive oil	2 tsp. lime juice

METHOD

Put the egg, garlic, mustard powder, and seasoning into a blender. Mix briefly, then with the motor still running, very slowly trickle in the oil. Transfer the sauce to a bowl and stir in the remaining ingredients.

Ginger and Green Onion Mayonnaise

MAKES ABOUT 1¼ CUPS

To make the ginger juice needed for this recipe, crush a piece of peeled ginger in a garlic press. Use to dress chicken, pork, fish or shellfish, and vegetable salads.

INGREDIENTS

2 egg yolks (see page 8)

salt

½–1 tsp ginger juice

½ cup olive oil

½ cup peanut oil

2 Tbsp. chopped green onions

freshly ground black pepper

METHOD

Put the egg yolks, salt, and ½ tsp. of ginger juice into a blender. Mix briefly. With the motor running, slowly trickle in the oils; add the green onions almost at the end so they become finely chopped but are not reduced to a pulp.

Season with black pepper. Add more ginger juice if necessary.

Sesame Seed and Garlic Mayonnaise

MAKES ABOUT 1½ CUPS

Rice vinegar is used for this recipe so the dressing is mild, getting its character from the green onions, roasted sesame seeds, and a little garlic (you can increase the garlic if liked). To roast sesame seeds, put them into a dry, heavy, small skillet and heat gently until they are light brown in color and smell toasted.

INGREDIENTS

2 egg yolks (see page 8)

2 garlic cloves

salt

2 tsp white rice vinegar

1 cup mild olive oil (or ½ cup olive oil and ½ cup peanut oil)

4 Tbsp. chopped green onions

1 Tbsp. sesame seeds, roasted

freshly ground black pepper

METHOD

Put the egg yolks, garlic, salt, and vinegar into a blender. Mix together briefly. With the motor running, slowly trickle in the olive oil; add the green onions almost at the end.

Transfer to a bowl. Fold in the sesame seeds and season with black pepper.

Curry Mayonnaise

MAKES ABOUT 1 CUP

Use for chicken, ham, egg, or potato salads, to liven up left over roast turkey, or in chicken, ham, or egg sandwiches.

INGREDIENTS

6 Tbsp. bottled or home-made mayonnaise (see page 19)

6 Tbsp. heavy cream

1 Tbsp. curry paste

1 Tbsp. shallot or red onion, finely chopped

juice of ½ lemon

1 Tbsp. mango chutney

salt and freshly ground black pepper

METHOD

Put all the ingredients into a bowl and stir together. Cover and let stand for at least 30 minutes.

LEFT *Sesame Seed and Garlic Mayonnaise*

6

SALAD DRESSINGS WITH YOGURT, CHEESE, AND CREAM

Yogurt, cream, and cheeses have a variety of tastes, consistencies and fat contents, so they can be used to add different flavors and textures to dressings. Yogurt can be used to lower the fat content, therefore calories and cholesterol of both the French dressing type and mayonnaise type. As well as adding richness to dressings, cream can also be used instead of oil; this is also less fattening than a dressing based on oil because, measure for measure, cream contains fewer calories.

Cream, curd, and ricotta cheeses make richer, thicker dressings than cream, while blue cheeses add piquancy.

For people who cannot tolerate, or prefer not to eat dairy products, a tofu-based mayonnaise is included at the end of the chapter.

Yogurt Vinaigrette

MAKES ABOUT 1½ CUPS

This is a lighter tasting, fresher alternative to ordinary vinaigrette, and can be used in the same ways. Walnut or hazelnut oil can be substituted for half of the olive oil, depending on the salad.

INGREDIENTS

6 Tbsp. plain yogurt	about 2 Tbsp. water (optional)
2 Tbsp. sherry vinegar	dash of fine granulated sugar
4 Tbsp. olive oil	salt and freshly ground white or black pepper
2 tsp. *Dijon* mustard	

METHOD

Put the yogurt, vinegar, oil, and mustard into a bowl and mix together. If the vinaigrette is too thick (thicknesses of yogurts vary), add a little water. Add sugar and seasoning to taste.

Yogurt Salad Dressing

MAKES ABOUT 1½ CUPS

An easy to make, light, fresh tasting dressing that will liven up green salads. For extra interest, add 1 oz. chopped fresh herbs such as chives, or mixed herbs. The dressing will not keep very long as the yogurt acts on the cream and turns it into rich yogurt.

INGREDIENTS

⅔ cup plain yogurt	dash of fine granulated sugar
3 cups heavy cream	salt and freshly ground white or black pepper
juice of 1 lemon	

METHOD

Put the yogurt, cream, and lemon juice into a bowl and stir together. Add sugar and seasoning to taste.

Mustard Yogurt Dressing

MAKES ABOUT 1¼ CUPS

A light but well-flavored dressing for spinach, potato, or other vegetable salads.

INGREDIENTS

1 cup plain yogurt

1 Tbsp. finely chopped green onion

1 Tbsp. *Dijon* mustard

1 Tbsp. chopped fresh parsley or chives

salt and pepper

METHOD

Put all the ingredients into a bowl and stir together until evenly mixed. Cover and chill before using.

Yogurt and Orange Dressing

MAKES ABOUT 1¼ CUPS

Use for first course fruit salads, such as melon and orange, and garnish with mint.

INGREDIENTS

3 Tbsp. orange juice

1 Tbsp. clear honey

1 cup thick plain yogurt

salt and freshly ground white pepper

METHOD

Stir the orange juice into the honey. Add the orange juice mixture to the yogurt and stir together. Season to taste. Cover and chill.

Yogurt and Tahini Dressing

MAKES ABOUT 1 CUP

I have had various versions of this dressing throughout the Middle East. Sometimes the ground cumin is omitted, sometimes chopped cilantro or paprika are added. Serve it with egg salads, as a dressing for coleslaw salad, with warm new potatoes, or crudités.

INGREDIENTS

3–4 tsp. lemon juice

6 Tbsp. plain yogurt

1–2 garlic cloves, finely minced

6 Tbsp. olive oil

4 Tbsp. tahini

dash of ground cumin

salt and freshly ground black pepper

METHOD

Whisk the lemon juice into the yogurt. Add the garlic. Slowly stir in the oil until well mixed.

Beat in the tahini then add ground cumin and seasoning to taste. Cover and chill before using.

Herby Cream Cheese Dressing

MAKES SCANT 1 CUP

Mixing buttermilk with soft cheese makes a dressing that is creamy but not too rich. The fresh flavors of the herbs also make it taste light. Use it for cooked vegetable salads or salads containing chicken.

INGREDIENTS

½ cup full fat soft cheese

⅔ cup buttermilk

1–2 tsp. lemon juice

4 Tbsp. chopped fresh mixed herbs or 2 Tbsp. chopped fresh tarragon or basil

salt and freshly ground black pepper

METHOD

Put the soft cheese into a bowl. Slowly pour in the buttermilk, stirring, until evenly blended. Add the lemon juice. Mix in the herbs. Season to taste. Serve chilled.

Warm Minted Lemon Cream Dressing

MAKES ABOUT ¾ CUP

To make a cold dressing, simply stir all the ingredients together. This is an ideal dressing for young, sweet peas, sugar snap peas, baby carrots and baby corn.

INGREDIENTS

4 Tbsp. crème fraîche or yogurt	5 Tbsp. plain yogurt
finely grated rind and juice of ½ lemon	salt and freshly ground black pepper
1 Tbsp. finely chopped or shredded fresh mint	

METHOD

Put the crème fraîche into a small saucepan and heat gently. Stir in the lemon rind and juice, and the mint. When warmed through, stir in the yogurt, taking care not to let the dressing overheat. Season to taste.

Oil-free Cream Vinaigrette

MAKES ABOUT 1¼ CUPS

Chill the dressing well and pour it over crisp lettuce leaves, or mix with cold cooked vegetables. Do not make the dressing too far in advance otherwise the vinegar will act upon the cream and thicken it.

INGREDIENTS

½ garlic clove	2 tsp. tarragon vinegar
salt and freshly ground white or black pepper	1 cup light cream
1 hard-cooked egg	dash of fine granulated sugar
½ tsp. *Dijon* mustard	

METHOD

Put the garlic into a mortar or a bowl, add a dash of salt and crush together to a paste.

Separate the egg white from the yolk; reserve the egg white for garnishing the salad. Add the egg yolk, mustard, and vinegar to the bowl and mix with the garlic. Stir in the cream and add sugar and pepper to taste. Cover and chill.

RIGHT *Warm Minted Lemon Cream Dressing*

Light Herb Sauce

MAKES ABOUT ¾ CUP

A simple, quick sauce that can be flavored with any herb. If you prefer a milder dressing, leave out the shallot. Serve the dressing over green salads, warm new potato salads, vegetable salads, or warm white beans such as navy or cannelini.

INGREDIENTS

⅔ cup sour cream, thick yogurt or plain yogurt	1 tsp. finely chopped shallot
2 Tbsp. chopped fresh herbs	salt and freshly ground white or black pepper

METHOD

Put the sour cream or yogurt, herbs, and shallot into a bowl. Stir together and season to taste.

Tofu Mayonnaise

MAKES ABOUT ¾ CUP

This delicious, creamy mayonnaise-style dressing is useful for vegans. It can be flavored with a little minced garlic, some chopped herbs, or a few drops of chili sauce. This mayonnaise can be kept in a covered container in the refrigerator for a few days.

INGREDIENTS

½ cup silken tofu	2 Tbsp. sunflower oil
2 tsp. lemon juice	salt and freshly ground black pepper
1 tsp. *Dijon* mustard	

METHOD

Put all the ingredients into a blender and mix until smooth.

Ricotta and Blue Cheese Dressing

MAKES ABOUT 2 CUPS

A cheese with some piquancy is best for this dressing to contrast with the creaminess of the ricotta cheese. The dressing can be flavored with garlic, green onions, or herbs such as parsley, rosemary, or sage. Use for warm pasta, potato, rice, lima or cannelini beans, or green lentil salads, or over crisp lettuce leaves.

INGREDIENTS

5 oz. ricotta cheese

5 oz. Stilton or other blue cheese such as Gorgonzola or Roquefort

5 oz. crème fraîche or thick yogurt

salt and freshly ground black pepper

METHOD

Crumble the ricotta and blue cheese into a bowl and mash lightly together with a fork. Slowly pour in the crème fraîche, mixing well with a fork until the dressing is smooth. Season with a little salt and plenty of black pepper.

Creamy Mustard Vinaigrette

MAKES ABOUT ½ CUP

Tarragon and fennel seeds give complexity to the flavor of this powerful dressing, while crème fraîche smooths the flavor with piquant creaminess. The vinaigrette is great over white bean and robust lettuce leaf salads, potato salads, cheese salads, eggs, or with beef.

INGREDIENTS

¼ tsp. fennel seeds	salt
1 tsp. tarragon leaves	2 Tbsp. crème fraîche or sour cream
½ tsp. *Dijon* mustard	
1½ Tbsp. sherry vinegar	6 Tbsp. olive oil

METHOD

Put the fennel seeds into a bowl and crush with the end of a rolling pin. Add the tarragon and crush lightly.

Stir the mustard, vinegar, salt, and crème fraîche into the bowl. Slowly pour in the oil, whisking until well emulsified.

Creamy Watercress Dressing

MAKES ABOUT ¾ CUP

You can use all heavy cream or crème fraîche, or dilute either with some yogurt in whatever proportions you like, but keep at least 2 Tbsp. cream or crème fraîche for some creaminess and body. Alternatively, use thick yogurt for a creamy taste but not too many calories. Sour cream could also be used. Serve over bean, rice, or potato salads, with cold salmon, trout, chicken or eggs, or in egg sandwiches.

INGREDIENTS

large handful of watercress leaves	squeeze of lemon juice (optional)
¾ cup heavy cream or crème fraîche, or a mixture of either and plain yogurt, thick yogurt, or sour cream	salt and freshly ground white or black pepper

METHOD

Add the watercress leaves to a saucepan of boiling water and boil for 1 minute. Drain and rinse under running cold water. Drain well and dry thoroughly.

Put the watercress into a blender and add the cream, crème fraîche and/or yogurt. Mix to a green purée. Season to taste.

Yogurt and Curd Cheese "Mayonnaise"

MAKES ABOUT ⅔ CUP

The taste of this low-fat version of mayonnaise is not too far removed from the real thing. It can be flavored in the same way as mayonnaise with garlic, mustard, herbs etc, and served in place of mayonnaise. A little milk can be added to thin the mayonnaise if liked.

INGREDIENTS

½ cup medium fat curd cheese or medium fat soft cheese

2 Tbsp. plain yogurt

2 tsp. olive oil

½ tsp. white wine vinegar

salt and freshly ground black pepper

METHOD

Put the cheese into a bowl. Stir in the yogurt, oil, and vinegar until smooth. Season to taste. Chill before serving.

Horseradish and Sour Cream Dressing

MAKES ABOUT 1 CUP

Spoon this dressing over sliced tomatoes, toss with boiled cauliflower for an inspired salad, or serve with sliced cold beef.

INGREDIENTS

¾ cup sour cream

4 Tbsp. grated fresh or bottled horseradish

2 tsp. lemon juice or white wine vinegar

salt and freshly ground black pepper

METHOD

Pour the sour cream into a bowl. Stir in the horseradish and lemon juice or white wine vinegar to taste. Season to taste. Cover and chill.

7

SWEET DRESSINGS
AND MARINADES

Dressings and marinades can be used to quickly
and easily add a special touch to fruits that are to
be served for dessert. The same recipe can even
sometimes double as both a marinade and a dressing
(see page 93).

Spices are often included in sweet dressings and
marinades because they harmonize with fruits and
enhance their sweet fruitiness. Wine always makes a
dish seem more luxurious. Using it as a marinade or
dressing is the quickest and most simple way I know
of making a dessert that I'm sure will impress, yet will
be light and fresh-tasting, unlike so many "impressive"
desserts which are very rich and calorie-laden.

White Wine Marinade

MAKES ABOUT 1½ CUPS

This is a light summery marinade that combines well with oranges, melons, peaches, and pineapples. Pour it over the fruit while it is hot and leave the fruit to steep until cold.

INGREDIENTS

1¼ cups medium bodied dry white wine	long strip of lemon or lime peel
¼ cup sugar	6 lemon balm leaves
	dash of ground mace

METHOD

Pour the wine into a saucepan. Add the sugar, lemon or lime peel, lemon balm leaves, and mace and heat gently, stirring until the sugar has dissolved. Bring to a boil and bubble for 1 minute.

Cardamom Butter Dressing

MAKES ABOUT 1 CUP

This fragrant buttery dressing spiked with Scotch or brandy adds a special air of luxury to fruit kebabs or chunks or wedges of fruit that are going to be broiled; my favorite fruits for this treatment are tropical fruits such as pineapples, mangoes, papayas, bananas, or pears. For a variation, use 2½ Tbsp. finely chopped fresh ginger instead of cardamom.

INGREDIENTS

½ cup unsalted butter, diced	2 Tbsp. Scotch or brandy
seeds from 6 cardamom pods, crushed	2 Tbsp. icing sugar
2 Tbsp. lime or orange juice	

METHOD

Melt the butter in a small saucepan over a low heat. Stir in the remaining ingredients until evenly blended.

Strawberry Wine Marinade

This simple but sophisticated marinade is just right for making an easy but impressive light dessert of pears, plums, peaches, apricots, cherries, lychees, or mangosteens.

INGREDIENTS

4 Tbsp. sugar

2½ cups medium bodied dry white wine

4 large ripe strawberries

METHOD

Put the sugar and wine in a wide, shallow saucepan and heat gently, stirring until the sugar has dissolved. Bring to a boil and boil gently, without stirring, for 3–4 minutes.

Add the strawberries to the pan and simmer for 6–7 minutes until reduced by half and syrupy. Pour over the prepared fruit and let cool. Chill before serving.

Orange, Lemon, and Honey Dressing

MAKES ABOUT ¾ CUP

A favorite simple, light summer dessert is made by pouring this dressing over melon balls (preferably a combination of different melons) or cubes, orange or grapefruit slices, peaches, or strawberries, then covering and chilling.

INGREDIENTS

½ cup orange juice	about 2 Tbsp. clear honey, or to taste
2 Tbsp. lemon juice	

METHOD

Pour the orange and lemon juices into a bowl. Add the honey and stir until melted.

Red Wine Marinade

MAKES ABOUT 1½ CUPS

Pour the hot marinade over sliced ripe pears, halved and pitted ripe plums, strawberries, or halved and pitted ripe peaches. If the fruit is not ripe enough to eat as it is, it can be cooked in the marinade until tender before leaving it to steep.

INGREDIENTS

1¼ cups red wine	¼ tsp. freshly grated nutmeg
⅓ cup soft brown sugar	
long strip of orange peel	2 inch piece of cinnamon
1 tsp. ground mixed spices	5 cloves

METHOD

Pour the wine into a saucepan. Add the sugar, orange peel, and spices and heat gently, stirring, until the sugar has dissolved. Bring to a boil and bubble for 1 minute.

Sweet Ginger, Cinnamon, and Rice Wine

MAKES ABOUT ⅔ CUP MARINADE; ABOUT ¼ CUP DRESSING

I use this recipe both as a marinade and a dressing for broiled fruits – first steep the fruit in it, then remove the fruit and broil it. Boil the dressing that is left until it is syrupy and brush over the hot fruit. Decorate the fruit with extra chopped candied ginger and serve with lime or lemon wedges.

INGREDIENTS

½ cup rice wine	1 Tbsp. finely chopped candied ginger
2 Tbsp. grated fresh ginger	½ cinnamon stick
	dash of sugar

METHOD

Put all the ingredients into a small saucepan and bring just to boiling point. Pour over the fruit and let cool. Using a slotted spoon, scoop out the fruit. Strain the marinade into a small saucepan and boil until syrupy.

Broil the fruit until lightly browned then pour over the ginger and rice wine syrup.

Spiced Citrus Syrup

MAKES ABOUT 2 CUPS

This syrup is for pouring over fruit salads, and is particularly good with tropical fruits such as mangoes and papayas, melons, oranges, pears, and grapes.

INGREDIENTS

1¼ cups water	½ tsp. ground ginger
½ cup sugar	1 cinnamon stick
2 large strips of lime or lemon rind	lime or lemon juice to taste
2 large strips of orange rind	

METHOD

Pour the water into a saucepan, add the sugar and heat gently, stirring until the sugar has dissolved. Add the fruit rinds, ginger, and cinnamon and bring slowly to a boil. Remove from the heat, cover and leave until cold. Chill.

Before using, strain the syrup and add lime or lemon juice to taste.

Ginger Dressing

MAKES ABOUT 1½ CUPS

Tropical fruit salads, containing, for example, lychees, mangoes, pineapple or papaya, oranges, clementines and tangerines, grapefruits, and pears marry particularly well with this dressing.

INGREDIENTS

¼ cup superfine sugar

⅔ cup water

⅔ cup ginger wine

2 pieces stem ginger preserved in syrup, finely chopped

finely grated rind and juice of 1½ limes

METHOD

Put the sugar and water into a saucepan and heat gently, stirring, until the sugar has dissolved. Bring to a boil then simmer for 1 minute without stirring. Remove the pan from the heat and add the ginger wine, chopped stem ginger, and lime rind and juice.

Pour over the prepared fruit and let cool. Chill before serving.

8

MARINADES
AND SPICE RUBS

Marinades can be simple or complex, or anywhere between the two. They can be light with just a light flavor, or they can be richly flavored with exotic spices from many different cuisines around the world.

Whatever ingredients you are using, including the oils, herbs, and spices, make sure they are fresh because even a slight stale or off flavor will penetrate the food to be marinated, so spoiling it.

The flavor of marinades will improve if they are left to sit for 30 minutes or more. Marinades can be made in advance and kept in an airtight container in the refrigerator for a few days.

Herb Marinade

MAKES ABOUT ⅔ CUP

This is a universal, versatile marinade that can be used for meat, poultry, fish, or vegetables. Be sure to use a well-flavored olive oil. The herbs can be varied according to the food that is to be marinated and what is available.

INGREDIENTS

4 Tbsp. olive oil	4 Tbsp. chopped fresh herbs
2 Tbsp. lemon or lime juice or white wine vinegar	freshly ground black pepper
1 garlic clove, minced	

METHOD

Mix all the ingredients together.

Orange and Herb Marinade

MAKES ABOUT 1¼ CUPS

White wine adds a special flavor to this marinade and therefore the foods marinated in it. I use it for pork, chicken, Cornish game hens, duck, and lamb.

INGREDIENTS

juice of 2 oranges	1 tsp. chopped fresh rosemary
⅔ cup dry white wine	1 garlic clove, minced
3 Tbsp. olive oil	freshly ground black pepper
1 tsp. chopped fresh marjoram	
1 tsp. chopped fresh thyme	

METHOD

Put all the ingredients into a bowl and whisk together.

Yogurt and Chile Marinade

MAKES ABOUT ¾ CUP

I use this marinade to spread over shelled large shrimp before broiling them. It can also be used for chicken kebabs.

INGREDIENTS

½ cup plain yogurt

1 onion, finely chopped

2 garlic cloves

2 fresh red chiles, seeded and chopped

juice of 1 lime

chile powder (optional)

salt and freshly ground black pepper

METHOD

Put the yogurt, onion, garlic, chiles, and lime juice in a blender. Mix to a paste. Add chile powder if liked, and season to taste.

Marinade for Broiled Vegetables

MAKES ABOUT ¾ CUP

Steep the broiled vegetables in this marinade, overnight at room temperature then serve as an anti-pasta, a first course accompanied by good, firm bread to mop up the juices, or as part of a buffet.

INGREDIENTS

8 Tbsp. olive oil

1 Tbsp. sherry vinegar

1 garlic clove, minced

1 shallot, finely chopped

1 fresh red chili, seeded and finely chopped

salt and freshly ground black pepper

METHOD

Put all the ingredients into a bowl and mix together.

Souvlakia Marinade

MAKES ABOUT ⅔ CUP

Souvlakia, tasty broiled or barbecued lamb kebabs that are usually served with yogurt trickled over, in split pitta breads, are sold throughout Greece by street vendors, cafés, and restaurants.

INGREDIENTS

4 garlic cloves

1 onion

1 tsp. ground cumin

1 tsp. cayenne pepper or a few drops of Tabasco sauce

¼ cup olive oil

freshly ground black pepper

METHOD

Put the garlic and onion into a blender, add the spices and oil and mix until reduced to a slush. Season with black pepper.

RIGHT *Marinade for Broiled Vegetables*

Mandarin Marinade

MAKES ABOUT 1 CUP

This slightly sweet, yet sharp, citrus flavored marinade spiked with fresh ginger can be used with beef, lamb, pork, wild and reared duck, and pigeon.

INGREDIENTS

2 Tbsp. mandarin or orange marmalade

1 tsp. grated fresh ginger

1 garlic clove, minced

¼ cup white wine vinegar

¼ cup orange juice

¼ cup lemon juice

½ cup olive oil

freshly ground black pepper

METHOD

Put all the ingredients except the oil and seasoning in a saucepan and heat, stirring, until the marmalade has melted. Simmer until reduced to ½ cup. Pour into a bowl and let cool.

Stir in the oil and season with black pepper to taste.

Lime and Pernod Marinade

MAKES ABOUT 1 CUP

Lime marries well with the anise flavor of Pernod to make a marinade that is ideal for seafood, especially large, raw shrimp and scallops, and thick pieces of fresh haddock.

INGREDIENTS

4 Tbsp. Pernod

juice of 2 limes

1 small garlic clove, minced (optional)

1 tsp. fennel seeds, lightly crushed

1½ Tbsp. chopped fresh cilantro

5 Tbsp. olive oil

freshly ground black pepper

METHOD

Put all the ingredients into a bowl and stir together.

Cilantro, Lime, and Vermouth Marinade

MAKES ABOUT ¾ CUP

Dry white vermouths are flavored with blends of herbs and spices. As each producer has their own special blend, the taste (and quality) of vermouths varies between brands. If you would like to add a bit of "heat", add a drop or two of Tabasco sauce.

INGREDIENTS

3 Tbsp. chopped fresh cilantro

finely grated rind and juice of 2 limes

2 Tbsp. dry white vermouth

2 garlic cloves, minced

¼ cup olive oil

Tabasco sauce (optional)

freshly ground black pepper

METHOD

Put all the ingredients into a bowl and mix together.

Salmoriglio

MAKES ABOUT 1¼ CUPS

In Sicily, salmoriglio is used as the marinade for fish that is to be broiled or barbecued, usually threaded onto skewers. Sicilians believe that the only way to make a really good salmoriglio is to add seawater; in the absence of this ingredient use sea salt for seasoning. Salmoriglio can also be served warm as a sauce to accompany the fish.

INGREDIENTS

1 garlic clove	¾ cup virgin olive oil, warmed slightly
1 Tbsp. finely chopped fresh parsley	3 Tbsp. hot water
1½ tsp. chopped fresh oregano	about 4 Tbsp. lemon juice
about 1 tsp. chopped fresh rosemary	sea salt and freshly ground black pepper

METHOD

Put the garlic, the herbs and a dash of salt into a mortar or bowl and pound to a paste with a pestle or the end of a rolling pin.

Pour the oil into a warm bowl then, using a fork, slowly pour in the hot water followed by the lemon juice, whisking constantly until well emulsified. Add the herb and garlic mixture, and black pepper to taste.

Put the bowl over a saucepan of hot water and warm for 5 minutes, whisking occasionally. Let cool before using.

Yogurt and Sun-dried Tomato Marinade

MAKES ABOUT ¾ CUP

This is a very simple yet effective marinade to spread over salmon, trout, or chicken. Ground spices such as cumin and cardamom can be added for a spicy flavor, if liked.

INGREDIENTS

⅔ cup plain yogurt	1 Tbsp. lemon juice
1 large garlic clove, minced	1 Tbsp. sun-dried tomato paste
finely grated rind of 1 lemon	freshly ground black pepper

METHOD

Put the yogurt into a bowl. Add the remaining ingredients and stir together.

LEFT *Salmoriglio*

Orange and Honey Marinade

MAKES ABOUT 2 CUPS

A simple but very effective marinade for barbecued spare ribs; it also works well with pork chops and steaks.

INGREDIENTS

1¼ cups pure orange juice from a carton

3 Tbsp. clear honey

2 Tbsp. lemon juice

1 Tbsp. soy sauce

3 Tbsp. Worcestershire sauce

METHOD

Pour the orange juice into a saucepan, add the honey and heat gently, stirring, until the honey has dissolved.

Remove from the heat, add the remaining ingredients and let cool.

Orange and Ginger Marinade

MAKES ABOUT 1¾ CUPS

Soy sauce adds depth and richness to the orange juice, lemon juice adds a tang and grated fresh ginger gives a zesty flavor, all of which combine to make this an ideal marinade for giving distinction to chicken, duck, turkey, and pork.

INGREDIENTS

scant 1 cup orange juice

4 Tbsp. lemon juice

1 Tbsp. grated fresh ginger

4 Tbsp. light soy sauce

1 Tbsp. white wine vinegar

4 Tbsp. dry sherry

1 plump garlic clove, minced

freshly ground black pepper

METHOD

Put all the ingredients into a bowl and whisk together.

Dried Apricot Marinade

MAKES ABOUT 1 CUP

Curry powder adds an appetizing spicy note to the deep fruit flavor of dried apricots to make a marinade that transforms lamb, whole chicken or chicken portions with skin, pork, or duck.

INGREDIENTS

⅔ cup dried apricots, soaked overnight

2 Tbsp. olive oil

1 large onion, sliced

1 garlic clove, finely chopped

1½ tsp. curry powder

1½ Tbsp. white wine vinegar

1½ Tbsp. lemon juice

dash of cayenne pepper

1½ tsp. sugar

freshly ground black pepper

METHOD

Put the apricots into a small saucepan and add enough of their soaking liquid to just cover. Bring to a boil then simmer gently for 15–20 minutes or until tender.

Let cool slightly, tip into a blender and mix to a purée.

Heat the oil in a skillet, add the onion and garlic and fry until softened and golden. Stir in the curry powder for 1 minute then add the apricot purée and remaining ingredients. Stir well. Bring to a boil then let cool.

Coconut Marinade

MAKES ABOUT 1 CUP

This Far-Eastern style marinade works well with firm fish such as monkfish, or with chicken, turkey, pork, or lamb.

INGREDIENTS

⅔ cup boiling water

3 oz. creamed coconut

1 tsp. lime juice

1 shallot, finely chopped

1 garlic clove, finely chopped

1 lemon grass stalk, thoroughly crushed

the seeds from 3 cardamom pods, crushed

½ inch piece of fresh ginger, grated

½ tsp ground cumin

freshly ground black pepper

METHOD

Pour the boiling water over the coconut and stir until smooth. Add the remaining ingredients and cool.

Green Peppercorn, Mustard, and Parsley Marinade

MAKES ABOUT 1 CUP

A spicy mustard paste to spread thickly over thick lamb steaks and lamb chops to give them a real lift.

INGREDIENTS

1 Tbsp. green peppercorns, finely chopped

4 Tbsp. wholegrain mustard

3 Tbsp. white and green parts of green onions

½ cup fresh bread crumbs

3 Tbsp. chopped fresh parsley

¼ tsp. cayenne pepper

1 Tbsp. corn oil

METHOD

Put the peppercorns, mustard, green onions, bread crumbs, parsley, and cayenne pepper into a bowl and stir together thoroughly. Stir in the oil a drop at a time to make a thick paste.

Yogurt and Mint Marinade

MAKES ABOUT ½ CUP

Mint is married to lamb in the Middle East as well as in England. Here it is combined with thick, creamy yogurt to produce meltingly tender lamb kebabs, broiled lamb chops and steaks, and roast lamb. The marinade also works well with chicken and turkey.

INGREDIENTS

6 Tbsp. rich yogurt

1 garlic clove, minced

about 2 Tbsp. chopped fresh mint

freshly ground black pepper

METHOD

Stir all the ingredients together.

Spiced Yogurt Marinade

MAKES ABOUT ¾ CUP

This is one of my favorite marinades to use for chicken drumsticks and thighs that are to be broiled, or, better still, barbecued. It can also be used for fish or lamb.

INGREDIENTS

⅔ cup plain yogurt	2 tsp. paprika pepper
2 garlic cloves	½ tsp. ground chile
1 Tbsp. chopped fresh ginger	½ tsp. ground cardamom
1 Tbsp. ground cumin	

METHOD

Put all the ingredients into a blender and mix together until smooth.

Yogurt and Herb Marinade

MAKES SCANT 1 CUP

The herbs can be varied depending on which type of meat or poultry is being used, for example tarragon, thyme, sage, or lemon balm go with chicken; rosemary, tarragon, thyme, or mint with lamb; rosemary or parsley with beef; sage or bay with pork.

INGREDIENTS

4 Tbsp. olive oil	2 garlic cloves, minced
⅔ cup plain yogurt	freshly ground black pepper
about 4 Tbsp. chopped fresh herbs	

METHOD

Put all the ingredients into a bowl and mix together.

ABOVE *Spiced Yogurt Marinade*

Apple, Lemon, and Ginger Marinade

MAKES ABOUT ¾ CUP

This tangy, fruity dressing makes a good marriage with chicken, turkey, duck, or pork.

INGREDIENTS

6 Tbsp. unsweetened apple juice

3 lemon slices, finely chopped

¾ inch piece of fresh ginger, grated

1 garlic clove, minced

3 Tbsp. dry sherry

3 Tbsp. soy sauce

METHOD

Put all the ingredients into a bowl and mix together.

Sherry, Soy, Ginger, Cilantro, and Star Anise Marinade

MAKES ABOUT 1½ CUPS

When I want to give a change from plain roast lamb, pork, or beef, I marinate the joint in this recipe; the subtle, complex flavors give the meat a really special taste. I have also used the marinade for mature pheasants that are to be casseroled or braised.

INGREDIENTS

⅔ cup dry or medium sherry

⅔ cup soy sauce

1 inch piece of fresh ginger, grated

4 garlic cloves, minced

2 Tbsp. chopped fresh cilantro

2 Tbsp. clear honey

3 star anise, lightly crushed

METHOD

Put all the ingredients into a bowl and mix together.

Tandoori Marinade

MAKES ABOUT 2 CUPS

This is an authentic-tasting tandoori marinade for skinned chicken portions, cubes of lamb, raw jumbo shrimp peeled but with the heads left on, or firm-fleshed fish.

INGREDIENTS

1 onion, coarsely chopped

4 large garlic cloves

1 oz. fresh ginger

4 Tbsp. lemon juice

1 cup plain yogurt

4 Tbsp. sunflower oil

1 Tbsp. ground turmeric

1 Tbsp. ground coriander

1 tsp. ground cumin

½ tsp. ground cinnamon

½ tsp. grated nutmeg

½ tsp. freshly ground
black pepper

¼ tsp. ground cloves

¼ tsp. chile powder or
cayenne pepper

METHOD

Put the onion, garlic, and ginger into a blender and process until chopped. Add the remaining ingredients and mix until smooth.

Thai-style Marinade

MAKES ABOUT ¾ CUP

Here, typical ingredients of the Thai cuisine produce a well-flavored marinade that I have used with great success for broiled tuna, salmon, or swordfish steaks, firm white fish such as monkfish and cod, and chicken.

INGREDIENTS

2 garlic cloves, minced

1 fresh green chile, seeded and finely chopped

2 Tbsp. chopped cilantro

2 Tbsp. chopped basil

2 Tbsp. chopped mint

½ inch piece of fresh ginger, grated

¼ cup lime juice

1 Tbsp. fish sauce

1 Tbsp. sesame oil

freshly ground black pepper

METHOD

Put all the ingredients into a bowl. Stir together until well mixed.

Hoisin Sauce Marinade

MAKES ABOUT ¾ CUP

Hoisin sauce is a thick, slightly sweet, smooth Chinese bean sauce with a mild garlic taste. It is now widely available in supermarkets as well as Chinese food stores. Used in this recipe, hoisin sauce makes a marinade that adds a touch of distinction to chicken and pork without overpowering it.

INGREDIENTS

6 Tbsp. hoisin sauce	2 tsp. chopped fresh thyme
4 Tbsp. rice wine	freshly ground black pepper
2 Tbsp. olive oil	

METHOD

Put all the ingredients into a bowl. Stir together.

Spiced Sesame Oil Marinade

MAKES ABOUT ½ CUP

You will get quite different results whether you use lime or lemon juice. Either way, this marinade is good for pork, chicken, fish, or shellfish.

INGREDIENTS

1 plump garlic clove, finely chopped	1 Tbsp. sesame oil
2 green onions, finely chopped	2 Tbsp. groundnut oil
½ inch fresh ginger, grated	2 Tbsp. sake or dry sherry
	1 Tbsp. lemon or lime juice

METHOD

Put all the ingredients into a bowl. Whisk together.

Golden Escabeche Marinade

MAKES ABOUT 1½ CUPS

The name "escabeche" is derived from the Perso-Arabic word "sikbaj" which means "vinegar stew" and is applied, particularly in Spain and Mexico, to dishes of meat, poultry, game, or fish that are cooked then steeped in an acid-based marinade to help extend their edible shelf-life. With modern freezing and refrigeration techniques this practice is no longer necessary but escabeche dishes are so good to eat that they are still prepared. This is my all-time favorite escabeche marinade.

INGREDIENTS

large dash of saffron strands

3 Tbsp. medium bodied dry white wine, or hot water

2 Tbsp. virgin olive oil

2 red onions, thinly sliced

1½ tsp. cumin seeds, lightly crushed

½ tsp dried chile flakes

2 red peppers, sliced

finely grated rind and juice of 1 orange

juice of 1 lemon

dash of sugar

salt and freshly ground black pepper

METHOD

Soak the saffron strands in the wine or water for 5 minutes.

Heat the olive oil in a skillet, add the onions and cook for 2 minutes. Stir in the cumin seeds and chile flakes for about 45 seconds then add the red peppers. Fry, stirring occasionally, until soft. Add the saffron liquid, orange rind and juice, and the lemon juice. Bubble for a few minutes then add sugar and seasoning to taste. Let cool.

Curry Marinade

MAKES SCANT 1 CUP

Add an appetizing curry flavor to broiled chicken and turkey with this marinade. The strength of the curry flavor can be adjusted by altering the amount of curry powder or garam masala that is added, or using a hotter curry powder.

INGREDIENTS

5 Tbsp. white wine vinegar

½ cup olive oil

1 garlic clove, minced

1 tsp. curry powder or garam masala

freshly ground black pepper

METHOD

Put all the ingredients into a bowl and whisk together.

RIGHT *Golden Escabeche Marinade*

Saffron and Lemon Marinade

MAKES ABOUT ¾ CUP

Saffron and lemon combine to make an elegant marinade that originated in Italy. It is used for zucchini and large shrimp, but is also worth trying with scallops, firm white fish, or chicken breasts. Two tablespoons of chopped capers can be added for an additional piquant flavor.

INGREDIENTS

dash of saffron threads

1 Tbsp. hot water

2 garlic cloves, minced

juice of 1½ lemons

2 Tbsp. white wine vinegar

generous ½ cup mild olive oil

freshly ground black pepper

METHOD

Put the saffron in a bowl, pour over the water and let steep for 5 minutes. Add the remaining ingredients. Whisk together.

Fennel Marinade

MAKES ABOUT ½ CUP

The fresh aniseed flavor of fennel works particularly well with pork and is also effective with rabbit and chicken.

INGREDIENTS

1 garlic clove

seeds from 1 star anise

4 Tbsp. chopped fennel leaves

2 Tbsp. olive oil

METHOD

Put the garlic and star anise seeds into a mortar or bowl and crush together with a pestle or the end of a rolling pin. Add the fennel leaves, crush these a few times, then trickle in the oil, crushing to make a paste.

Satay Marinade

MAKES ABOUT ½ CUP

Satays are ubiquitous throughout South East Asia so you will find many different recipes for satays themselves and for the marinades and sauces that accompany them. This is one of my favorite satay marinades that I use for satays of pork, chicken, or large shrimp. Serve with Indonesian Peanut Dressing (see page 51).

INGREDIENTS

4 Tbsp. coconut milk

1 Tbsp. soft dark brown sugar

1 garlic clove, finely chopped

2 tsp. ground coriander

2 tsp. ground cumin

1 tsp. ground turmeric

squeeze of lemon juice

METHOD

Mix all the ingredients together to make a fairly dry paste. Spoon over the ingredients to be marinated and rub the marinade thoroughly over them.

White Wine Marinade

MAKES ABOUT 1¼ CUPS

Lighter than a red wine marinade, this recipe is suitable for farmed pigeon and rabbit, young partridge and pheasant, lamb, and chicken, turkey, and pork when you want a more robust dish.

INGREDIENTS

2 Tbsp. mild olive oil	2 parsley stems
1 shallot, finely chopped	1 bay leaf, torn
1 carrot, finely chopped	1 sprig of thyme
2 juniper berries, crushed	1 slice of lemon
2 black peppercorns, crushed	about 1¼ cups medium bodied dry white wine
1 sprig of celery leaves, chopped	

METHOD

Put all the ingredients into a bowl and stir. If the meat is not covered by the marinade, add some more wine.

Devilled Marinade

MAKES ABOUT ¾ CUP

The use of the name "devilled" indicates that it is highly seasoned with a hot ingredient such as mustard. Spread onto chicken portions with skin, turkey, lamb, or beef.

INGREDIENTS

4 Tbsp. tomato catsup	4 tsp. ground turmeric
1 Tbsp. lemon juice	1 Tbsp. English mustard powder
1 Tbsp. paprika pepper	¼ cup unsalted butter, chopped
4 tsp. ground cumin	

METHOD

Put the tomato catsup and lemon juice into a bowl. Stir in the paprika, cumin, turmeric, and mustard powder.

Put the butter into a small saucepan and heat gently until just melted. Stir the butter into the spice mixture until evenly combined.

Mexican Marinade

MAKES ABOUT ⅔ CUP

A hot and lightly spicy marinade that is most suitable for pork, but also can be used for chicken, turkey, lamb, or beef.

INGREDIENTS

2 garlic cloves, minced	¼ tsp. ground cumin
2 fresh red or green chiles, seeded and chopped	dash of ground cloves
	5 Tbsp. white wine vinegar
¼ tsp. dried thyme	freshly ground black pepper

METHOD

Put all the ingredients into a bowl and stir together.

Cooked Red Wine Marinade

MAKES 1½ CUPS

Simmering the vegetables, spices, and herbs in the wine mellows their flavors and draws them into the wine (which is also concentrated by the simmering), so giving a marinade that has a richer, more well-rounded flavor than an uncooked marinade.

INGREDIENTS

¼ cup olive oil

1 small onion, chopped

2 garlic cloves, chopped

1 carrot, chopped

1 celery stalk, chopped

1¾ cups medium bodied red wine

¼ cup red wine vinegar

6 juniper berries, crushed

6 black peppercorns, crushed

1 bouquet garni

METHOD

Heat half the oil in a saucepan, add the onion, garlic, carrot, and celery and fry until soft but not browned. Add the wine, wine vinegar, juniper berries, peppercorns, and bouquet garni. Bring to a boil then simmer for 15–20 minutes until the vegetables are tender. Add the remaining oil, cover and let cool.

Uncooked Spiced Red Wine Marinade

MAKES ABOUT 1¼ CUPS

This marinade is quite sweet. Use it to flavor and tenderize beef, lamb, or pork.

INGREDIENTS

1 tsp. coriander seeds	½ tsp. dried chile flakes
1 tsp. cumin seeds	1 Tbsp. soft brown sugar
1–2 garlic cloves, minced	5 Tbsp. red wine
1 small onion, finely chopped	½ cup olive oil

METHOD

Heat the coriander and cumin seeds in a small heavy skillet and fry until fragrant, shaking the pan.

Pour into a bowl and add the remaining ingredients.

Uncooked Red Wine Marinade

MAKES ABOUT 1½ CUPS

Well-flavored with vegetables, spices, and herbs and boosted with port, this marinade produces tasty beef, young hare and venison, wild pigeon, and pheasant dishes.

INGREDIENTS

2 Tbsp. olive oil	2–3 parsley stems
1 onion, finely chopped	2 sprigs of thyme
2 garlic cloves, minced	2 bay leaves, torn
2 carrots, finely chopped	1 sprig of rosemary
1 celery stalk, finely chopped	½ cup port
6 juniper berries, crushed	about 1 cup red wine, or enough to cover meat
8 black peppercorns, crushed	

METHOD

Put all the ingredients into a bowl and mix together. If the meat is not covered by the marinade, add some more red wine.

Spice Rub for Meat

MAKES ABOUT 7 TBSP

I use this spice rub for beef, pork, and lamb.

INGREDIENTS

1 tsp. finely chopped fresh oregano	1 Tbsp. paprika pepper
1 tsp. fennel seeds, crushed	½ tsp. cayenne pepper
½ small garlic clove, finely chopped	freshly ground black pepper

METHOD

Put all the ingredients into a bowl and mix together.

Garlicky Spice Rub

MAKES ABOUT 5 TBSP

This spice rub is especially effective with lamb and pork but can also be enjoyed with chicken and turkey.

INGREDIENTS

1 tsp. dried thyme	1 dried bay leaf, crushed
4 garlic cloves, finely chopped	6 black peppercorns, crushed

METHOD

Put all the ingredients into a bowl and mix together.

Cajun Spice Rub

MAKES ABOUT 7 TBSP

In addition to dried herbs and ground cumin, this spice rub also contains onion and garlic. It is especially effective with red meats. Dried basil, sage, or fennel can be substituted for the dried thyme or oregano for a change.

INGREDIENTS

1 plump garlic clove	½ tsp. ground cumin
½ small onion, chopped	½ tsp. mustard powder
1 tsp. dried thyme	½ tsp. freshly ground black pepper
1 tsp. dried oregano	

METHOD

Put the garlic and onion into a mortar or small bowl and crush with a pestle or the end of a rolling pin. Mix in the remaining ingredients.

Spice Rub for Fish

MAKES ABOUT 9 TBSP

The lemon, tarragon, and basil in this recipe make it particularly suitable for fish.

INGREDIENTS

2 tsp. finely grated
lemon rind

1 tsp. dried tarragon,
finely chopped

1 tsp. dried basil,
chopped

½ small garlic clove,
finely chopped

1 Tbsp. paprika pepper

½ tsp. cayenne pepper

freshly ground black
pepper

METHOD

Put all the ingredients into a bowl and stir together.

Simple Spice Rub

MAKES ABOUT 3 TBSP

I like to use this simple spice rub only for large pieces of salmon or tuna.

INGREDIENTS

1 tsp. cumin seeds	seeds from 6 cardamom pods
1 tsp. coriander seeds	½ tsp. black peppercorns

METHOD

Heat a dry, small, heavy skillet, add all the seeds and heat until fragrant, shaking the pan frequently.

Tip the spices into a small blender, a spice grinder, mortar, or a bowl. Grind finely, or crush finely with the end of a rolling pin.

Spice Rub for Chicken and Turkey

MAKES ABOUT 7 TBSP

Being particularly herby, this spice rub really perks up chicken and turkey.

INGREDIENTS

1 tsp. dried tarragon, finely chopped	½ small garlic clove, finely chopped
¾ tsp. dried marjoram, finely chopped	1 Tbsp. paprika pepper
¼ tsp. dried thyme, finely chopped	½ tsp. cayenne pepper
¼ tsp. dried sage, finely chopped	freshly ground black pepper

METHOD

Put all the ingredients into a bowl and mix together.